'Charming, witty and sexy...impossible to put down. Harry's writing is profoundly moving, he handles the most complex conversations with the lightest of touches.' - **Laura Kay,** author of The Split, Tell Me Everything and Wild Things

* * *

'Harry's anger at how much further we have to go is only matched by the scale of his hope that, together, we'll get there - and in this memoir Harry is showing us the way. A miracle.' - **Adam Zmith,** author of Deep Sniff, Polari Prize Winner 2022

* * *

'A rallying cry for liberation and an intimate self-reflection, Nicholas celebrates and examines queer masculinity in its various forms, the good, the bad and the ugly. A book with something for all of us.' - **David Chipakupaku,** journalist

* * *

'This singular exploration of one man's journey towards himself shows us we are infinitely distinct and unique, and all the stronger as a community for it.' - **Andrew McMillan,** poet and author of 100 Queer Poems, Physical and Pandemonium

* * *

'Nicholas has written a revelatory, deeply generous memoir of queer existence and resistance. His message is empowered and empowering, sensitive and full of heart.' - **Peter Scalpello,** queer poet and author of Limbic

* * *

'Harry's vulnerability and honesty feel like an antidote in an increasingly hostile world. Beautiful.' - **Shivani Dave,** journalist and radio presenter

T0000401

'An engaging and easy-to-read book about a life experience that hardly anyone talks about.' – **Christine Burns MBE,** activist and author of *Trans Britain*

* * *

'Celebrates the interconnectedness and incongruity of gender, doing so in a way that frees the reader by extension. Will live on in the minds of each and every reader.' – **Neil Czeszejko,** Delphic Reviews

* * *

'Harry writes with such warmth and candour that he shines a light on the majesty of being exactly who you are – unapologetically. Without sugar-coating issues or hiding the hostility we face as a community, this book is a nuanced and individual look into the complexity of the trans experience within the wider LG-BTQIA+ community, a triumph.' – **Ben Pechey,** author, presenter and LGBTQIA+ advocate

* * *

'A beautifully important, eye-opening book' – **Daniel Harding,** author of *Gay Man Talking*

* * *

'Frank, funny, exciting and exploratory. I was absolutely glued to this. Incredible insight into how non-linear the trans journey can be; the way the world treats you differently based on your presentation, the sadness of letting go of previous spaces and the unique fear that goes with being thrust into a new community. As someone whose body also doesn't and may never conform to society's standards, I stan this book.' – **Fox Fisher,** author and activist

a trans man walks into a gay bar

a journey of self (and sexual) discovery

HARRY NICHOLAS

Jessica Kingsley Publishers
London and Philadelphia

of related interest

To Be A Trans Man
Our Stories of Transition,
Acceptance and Joy
Edited by Ezra Woodger
ISBN 978 1 78775 960 2
eISBN 978 1 78775 961 9

Queer Sex
A Trans and Non-Binary Guide to
Intimacy, Pleasure and Relationships
Juno Roche
ISBN 978 1 78592 406 4
eISBN 978 1 78450 770 1

Top To Bottom
A Memoir and Personal Guide
Through Phalloplasty
Finlay Games
ISBN 978 1 78775 587 1
eISBN 978 1 78775 588 8

Transitions
Our Stories of Being Trans
*Foreword by Meg-John Barker, Juno
Roche and Sabah Choudrey*
ISBN 978 1 78775 851 3
eISBN 978 1 78775 852 0

For all the trans people, the gender diverse people,
all the outsiders and the othered.

For my parents, Nigel and Janet. Thank you, for everything.

And to Liam, my home.

First published in Great Britain in 2023 by Jessica Kingsley Publishers
An imprint of John Murray Press

1

Copyright © Harry Nicholas 2023

The right of Harry Nicholas to be identified as the Author of the Work has been
asserted by him in accordance with the Copyright, Designs and Patents Act 1988.

Front cover image source: Sushil Nash https://unsplash.com/photos/LY--vxKePtE

Author photo source: Sophie Davidson https://www.sophie-davidson.co.uk

Content Warning:
This book mentions transphobia, homophobia and sexual assault.

A CIP catalogue record for this title is available from the British Library
and the Library of Congress

ISBN 978 1 83997 183 9
eISBN 978 1 83997 184 6

Printed and bound in Great Britain by TJ Books Limited

Jessica Kingsley Publishers' policy is to use papers that are natural, renewable
and recyclable products and made from wood grown in sustainable forests.
The logging and manufacturing processes are expected to conform to the
environmental regulations of the country of origin.

Jessica Kingsley Publishers
Carmelite House
50 Victoria Embankment
London EC4Y 0DZ

www.jkp.com

John Murray Press
Part of Hodder & Stoughton Limited
An Hachette UK Company

Contents

A Note from Harry

At the time I realized that I needed a book such as this one, I found that it didn't exist. One cold and dreary afternoon, I wandered, hair drenched and shoes soggy, into the Queen of bookshops – Gay's the Word – and toured their shelves. In contrast to the colourless, grey sky outside, Gay's the Word was full of rich and flavourful books, which gave me a kind of warm glow. Certainly, there was an abundance of books on gay love, trans experiences, memoirs, poetry, graphic novels, history and politics, but nothing, I thought, that would really help me. Not my situation, anyway. Then, I was a newly single, holy-shit-I-think-I'm-gay-now-what-do-I-do person, with little experience of dating or gay life as a man at all, really. Sat on the shelves, there were plenty of books about being gay, and much-needed, joyous accounts of what it is to be trans, but nothing really that encapsulated what it is to be both – to exist in the hazy terrain between.

I searched and searched, to find books, advice, videos... anything that would help me make sense of it all. But very little existed. And so I stumbled, often in the dark, trying to understand what it means to be a gay trans man – what space I can take up; how I can navigate sex and dating; whether I can ever love and be loved; how I can interpret my own masculinity, femininity and campness; how I can navigate (often) hypersexualized gay spaces; and ultimately, because so much of the world tells us we can't be, find out if I can be gay, trans and happy. I don't want you to be in any doubt, and it's not much of a 'spoiler' that the answer is YES. I am gay, trans and the happiest I've ever been. In fact, I didn't know it was possible for a person to be this happy. I have somehow managed to find a balance and understanding of my gender, sexuality and queerness which finally feels *right*. The things that once felt suffocating and confusing, now figured out, allow me to breathe more easily.

That isn't to say I don't have down days, or that my depression and anxiety, such as it is, doesn't continue to plague me to some degree. Far from it. Shit, we all have stuff going on. It just means that on an average Tuesday afternoon, walking to the bakery for lunch, I know I feel content with my identity – the part of me which has weighed so heavily, for so long, no longer chains me. Now, everything sits right and has its own place. I can look forward to the future and make plans.

Needless to say, this hasn't always been the case. As a teenager, I found it difficult to really think beyond being 18 because I just didn't know if I'd ever get to that point. I couldn't see *how* I would get there. I assumed that when my teachers said, 'Think about what you want to be when you grow up' or 'What do you want to do when you're older?' they meant a job or a partner or house and stuff. But I couldn't think past *boy*. If I wasn't a boy, there wasn't a future. So not knowing that transness was a 'thing' or that transitioning was even possible, a future seemed unreachable and it was impossible to picture myself within it. And so, I don't take this new-found happiness for granted. I cherish and embrace every moment.

The first thing you should know is that this is not a guidebook. I don't set out practical advice about how you can find happiness in your own life. Those types of books do exist, and if that's what you need in this moment, then please reach for them. I've included a list of books I've found useful and insightful at the back of this one if you need somewhere to start.

The second thing you should know is that this isn't a book on *how* to be gay and trans either. It would be impossible for me to write that given that there is no one way to be gay, trans and queer. We are a million people under one beautiful, horrifyingly-large-if-slightly-misshapen rainbow umbrella. **There is no right or wrong way to be gay and trans.** As many of the hideous and ill-fitting neon T-shirts tell you in that utterly condescending way they do, 'You do you, hun.'

So if this is not a guidebook to happiness or a how-to-be-gay-guide, what is it? Well, this is merely my own story. It's my scribbling. My messy working out. An attempt at trying to find the answers to my own questions and the questions other people expected me to immediately know the answers to. Questions like, 'Why, if you like boys, did you transition? Wouldn't it be easier to be a girl?' and, 'But if gay men like other men and you haven't had surgery, then will they want to...y'know...have sex with you?' and so on. I don't judge people for asking these questions of me. They are questions I've agonized over myself. I have at times wondered if it would have been easier to continue hiding as a girl and simply tried to squash down any dysphoria and live life as a straight woman as best I could. In fact, at 17, that's exactly what I decided to do. But in the end, none of us can deny our true selves. Not really. So this is the messy path to how I got to where I am – to the place that I know feels right as a gay trans man.

If you've ever wondered about the intersection between gender and sexuality – whether you're cis, trans, man, woman, non-binary, gay, straight, bi, ace, however you iden-tify – then I hope this book will offer some insight. And yes (word of warning to my parents, Nana, colleagues, ex-colleagues, brother, in-laws, pals, distant cousins, not-so-distant cousins), there are some rather raunchy, sexy bits in here too. Gay sex is *throws glitter* fabulous after all, and it would feel impertinent and wrong of me not to include sex in a book about gay love. After all, there is no shame in the sex we have, and so I won't shy away from talking about it here. This is not a book about being the acceptable face of gayness and transness, and it doesn't shy away from the horrible (and good) parts either. It's my truth about some of the joys of being a gay trans man and some of the difficulties too. If you're game for that, then welcome. This is a space for you to explore the answers to questions you may have wanted to ask but felt you couldn't, and it has been a space for me to ask these questions of myself. Or perhaps you don't have any questions at all; maybe you just liked the title. That's fine – we all judge books by their covers. If you've picked this book up, then thank you and I hope you can keep an open mind. I think the world would be a whole lot better if we took the time to learn and listen to people who are different to us.

Enough about what this book isn't and more about what it is. I've written this because we need a space to explore nu-anced, complex questions about gender and sexuality, without screaming at each other over Twitter. I wanted to look a little deeper into how these core parts of ourselves tangle and intertwine. I'm not saying I've got this all figured out, or that I'm right, or that I won't even change my mind on some of this stuff in the future. I just mean that these are important questions about what it means to be human – about our senses of self, our collective identities, our differences, our lust and our pleasure.

Arguably, this book is even more important now than when I first conceived of it. There is an uprising of a small but loud collective of LGB people who believe that the 'T' should be removed from the LGBTQ+ acronym. They intend to fracture our rainbow family. I, and so many others, have been concerned about this for some time, and it appears that this group is only getting louder and more persistent with terrifying and real consequences. Some members of this group say that being trans is a form of conversion therapy or that people who support trans rights are homophobic. In basic terms, they believe that trans men are actually confused women who experience misogyny so harshly that they decide they want to become men in order to escape it. They also say that trans women are groomers and paedophiles wanting to masquerade as women in order to abuse women in bathrooms and women-only spaces. Recently, I have been spat on and called a 'trans terrorist' and the 'biggest threat to modern society'. As a publicly out trans gay man I have been labelled a 'sex tourist', accused of 'committing rape by deception' and told that I am appropriating gay culture. This is not only directed at me though. You don't need look far to see these themes reflected in the British media. In fact, a quick Google search provides enough examples to last a lifetime. Leading these obscene and nauseating untruths are (some) lesbian, gay and bi people. These claims are coming from within our own community. So now, more than ever, we need solidarity, empathy, understanding and togetherness between LGBTQ+ people and our allies. We also need understanding that it's possible for us to exist as not only one letter. We exist not only as singular identities but at numerous cross-sections, which create differences and nuance. I, for example, along with many others, exist as gay, trans and queer, and I would like to celebrate and make room for a discussion about those intersections in this book.

Saying that 'I exist as' rather than the commonly used phrase 'I identify as' is important to me. 'I identify as' suggests that there is something to debate or there is something to uncover – that there is an untruth. As though it is something we believe about ourselves but others don't have to see, acknowledge or respect. We are currently faced with a political and societal landscape that tells us that trans people are not real, that we do not exist. For me, it is important to say 'I am gay and trans.' 'I do exist.' On trans rights protest marches I often see vibrantly designed placards that read 'trans women are women', 'trans men are men' and 'non-binary people are valid'. It's almost like we're telling ourselves, as well as those in opposition to our very existence, that we're real, because so much of the world tells us we aren't. And if you look closely, you'll notice that any attempt to convince the general public to support trans rights includes a personal narrative – a story of what it's *really* like to be trans. This wins empathy by humanizing us. The result, however, is that it demands we tell our stories, do away with any privacy and expose our vulnerability in order to prove that we deserve a very basic human right – the right to exist. I don't 'identify' as a gay man. I *am* a gay man, regardless of how other people may view me. I acknowledge that I am sharing my own story here, but I am doing so in the hope that you can see another perspective and to show what it is to live in the intersection between gender and sexuality. That, and I've always been an over-sharer.

Unfortunately, the combination of a hostile political environment, increasing momentum to remove the T from LGBTQ+, regular online pile-ons and a media war on trans people has left no room for nuance. There's no room to explain that trans lives are as expansive as they are complex and messy. We're scraping the barrel by asking for the acknowledgement we exist. Given how difficult it can be to speak (or write in my case) about anything trans at the moment, I have wondered if writing this is right thing to do. I have, on occasion, torn entire chapters up and been so close to throwing in the towel completely. I have been six months overdue on my writing deadline (...sorry Andrew) because it can be hard to make sense of the thoughts in my head while the outside noise is loud and unremitting. I thought maybe I should just try to get on with things, live quietly with my head bowed and behave. Perhaps there would be some queer resistance just in the act of living. But no. If ever there was a time to speak out about the terrain between being gay and trans, it is now. It is important for me, too, for all trans people, to say loudly, clearly and proudly that we exist. We are. We live. That we are messy, complex, friendly, nasty, sexy, domestic, boring, intelligent, kind, witty, geeky – human. So this is *my* resistance. My story. My unapologetic queer-ass humanity.

A few more disclaimers before we get into the real reason we're here. While I may mention some things in these pages that you may recognize or relate to, it is important for me to say that this book is *an* experience, not *the* experience.

Many gay trans men may have an entirely different worldview to me, and that is okay. I say this because as trans people we're not used to being given a stage to stand on or a microphone to speak into, and when we do, it can feel as though we're speaking on behalf of the entire trans community. It is important for me to say that I am not.

Lastly, if you cannot see a person like you (trans or otherwise) on the page, on the screen, on stage or online, I encourage you to write, sing, scream, Instagram, TikTok – whatever it may be – and share your story with the world. Our opulent and vast stories have been silenced for too long. It's time to make ourselves heard.

With love, and a call to action,

Harry

I'm Still Standin' (Yeah, Yeah, Yeah)

On a sunny Monday evening in mid-June of 2018, full of blossom and the promise of an eventful, scorching summer, my long-term girlfriend, Lucy, trundled along the Central line to my flat in West London. Lucy always worked long, almost torturous hours and left her office in Soho much later than I finished work. This could sometimes be frustrating if we were meeting for a drink or a dinner date in the evening, but on this occasion, it meant I had the time to cook us a homemade vegetarian lasagne. It turned out okay. And by that I mean to say it was terrible. It was clearly overcooked judging from the mass of flaking burnt bits, which looked like shards of soot that had escaped from an old fireplace, but at least I'd tried. I hid the burnt edges with spinach leaves fresh from the bag. The lasagne was a way of apology, I suppose, for whatever argument we'd had the weekend before. I think it was about me being ten minutes late (again) for the cinema. Or actually, now I come to think about it, maybe it was because Lucy had clocked my eyes lingering a little too long on a cute guy on the Tube, and just maybe, my face had flushed red... Anyway, whatever it was, we'd had an argument, Lucy had been away travelling for the weekend and now we were reuniting for the first time. I wanted to apologize, make amends over some questionable Italian cuisine and move on.

I imagine Lucy had a sweaty, anxiety-ridden journey full of planning, because moments after I opened the door and welcomed her into my bedroom, she broke up with me. It wasn't what I thought our breakup would look like. It wasn't a shouting match, or even an argument really. Lucy had arrived out of breath, either from the long uphill walk from the Tube station or because her anxiety was clearly flaring up – I didn't quite know which – and said with a knowing, sincere look on her face, 'Harry, I think we need to talk.' And we all know what *that* means.

I didn't say anything at first. I couldn't. I just looked at her blankly and wide-eyed, unable to process...well, anything, really. I could see her lips moving and could tell that sounds were escaping, but it was incomprehensible noise. I knew what all the words meant, but I failed to make sense of them. How could it be over? How could five years together end in a matter of moments and with only few sentences?

Lucy shared how she felt. She said that after being together since we were teenagers, she realized there was a queer world out there that she wanted to explore. I tried to interject and say, 'If an open relationship is something you'd like to consider, the—' but Lucy cut me off. She continued that she '...wanted to explore *alone*.' She wanted to experiment and find who she was away from me. And that we both knew that *really* I wanted to explore being gay, too, even if I wasn't ready to admit it at that point. She was doing this for the both of us, doing what I didn't have the courage to do, so we could have a chance to make sense of ourselves away from each other. It didn't matter that I cared for and loved her, or that she cared for and loved me too. Eventually, she said, that wouldn't be enough. My curiosity was bound to wander too... if it hadn't already. A knowing look. So it *was* the checking out of the guy on the Tube, I thought. I nodded, a numb ache beginning to burn in the keel of my stomach.

We sat on my bed for a while in silence. I could feel and hear my heart beating in my chest and I wanted it to stop. The heaviness in the air forced my neck down so I was looking at the floor, which offered no comfort. I thought about everything that the beige laminate floor in my tiny flat had seen: Lucy helping me move in a few years back after we'd graduated university, the rolling of our suitcases as we went on family holidays, our clothes adorning the floor as we stripped off in the sweltering summer evenings, arguments about Lucy not leaving her knitting needles and wool on the sofa *again*. Those moments felt so far away now, even if some of them were only a matter of weeks ago. I sighed heavily, hoping it would ease the ache that was beginning to burn more severely now. It didn't help. I breathed out again, my lip beginning to tremble, and I was surprised that I tasted blood. I realized then that I'd bitten into my lip in an effort to feel something real and present, because the breakup felt anything but.

After a long silence, and when I really couldn't look at the floor any longer, I arched my neck to look at Lucy, my eyes finding hers. I was surprised to see she'd been crying. I noticed the tears had made her brilliant blue eyes even more striking than usual, and I longed to hold her. To make it alright. We still loved each other; we both knew that. But Lucy was right. It wasn't enough. There was always 'something' missing. For me, it was a long-suppressed yearning for intimacy with men, for a romantic masculine presence. For Lucy, that longing may well have been for women. Lucy offered a hug and I accepted, her arms around me like a blanket. I noticed how well our bodies fitted against each other, as if they'd moulded themselves together in some way over the past few years. Our heads found their familiar places on each other's shoulders. Lucy had always said that my head was the perfect size to fit in the cul-de-sac of her shoulder, like our bodies had been made for each other's. We whispered to one another and agreed that we owed it to ourselves, and to each other, to at least try to give ourselves what we *really* wanted. We said it was an act of love to let each other go.

Lucy got up to leave, lifting her bulging work rucksack over her shoulder. She turned back to look at me and paused as if to say something more, but didn't. In that moment, we both realized there wasn't anything more to be said. She manoeuvred her way into the thin, badly lit corridor, and I heard the latch go on the front door.

Gone.

Her footsteps faded down the street and silence filled the space in my bedroom. Lucy was gone but her presence lingered. The heaviness that remained almost felt as if smoke had filled the room and grabbed my throat in a chokehold. I swallowed, my tongue dry as gravel. I tried to conjure tears but none came, and then I sat at the foot of my bed, feeling a kind of hung emptiness. I don't know how many hours passed. All I know was that it was dark when I finally shuffled into the kitchen and saw the lasagne that lay still uneaten on the worktop.

* * *

The breakup between me and Lucy was amicable, almost kind, but that didn't quash the sense of sickness, dread and loss that comes with any breakup. I often woke in my empty bed, still only sleeping on 'my side', a Lucy-sized empty space where she would usually be. Sometimes I'd wake spooning a pillow, subconsciously imagining it was her. When I would wake and open my eyes, I would have only a fleeting moment before remembering I was on my own. No more morning texts, no 'I can't wait to see you later', no more 'Do you want a cuppa?' It was those little things I missed most. As soon as I would remember I was on my own, I would wish I hadn't woken up at all.

I didn't eat. I couldn't stomach a thing. The lasagne left on the kitchen worktop remained there and mould began to creep over it. I couldn't face throwing it in the bin because, like some terrible metaphor, that really would mean it was all over. I found myself travelling mindlessly home from work, lying on my bed, staring at the walls and hoping the evening would close soon. The summer light that I'd been looking forward to all winter now felt like a visitor outstaying their welcome. I felt as though I couldn't go out because I wouldn't – couldn't – enjoy myself. Coming home to stare at the walls offered no comfort either. I didn't like going out, I didn't like staying in. It was the purest form of paralysis. My once-bursting colour-coded Google Calendar was now ghost-like and lacking. I didn't want to see friends. I didn't want to go to work. I didn't want to eat, go to the gym or look after myself. Any advice that well-intentioned family and friends would give would remain unread on my phone and redundant. It felt as if in losing her I'd also lost myself, and I had been left with a large emptiness that I was convinced I'd never be able to fill.

Lucy was great at many things, but timing, it turned out, wasn't one of them. It being June meant that London Pride was just around the corner. I knew the city streets would speak of bodies and of love and of colour and of togetherness and of rights. And when asked, our mutual friends spoke of already having plans – a cool lesbian night near Old Street that Lucy had suggested. I wasn't invited. Any other year I'd want to be front and centre at Pride, but my loneliness had emptied me in a way that only an escape into nature could fix, so my flatmate, Dan, and I decided to go on a road trip instead. Something as far away as we could manage. We found a campsite near Oxford that had specified that it allowed campfires (Dan's insistence) and that it had clean, 'proper' toilets and a shower room (mine). We drove onto the North Circular and headed out of London, in the opposite direction to that of my chosen family. Despite the traffic fumes and the summer heat, the air felt noticeably lighter.

The campsite was a tiny field at the bottom of a working farm and, as promised, there was a small toilet and shower hut and a large campfire circle in the centre of the site. A kind-looking outdoorsy couple were already sitting with their two strikingly well-behaved children, roasting marshmallows and sandwiching them between chocolate digestives. It was as if GO Outdoors had planted an advert for heterosexuality or something. It was bittersweet. Of course, it was nice to see families enjoying time together, but I wondered if now, as a single man for the first time in my life, I'd ever be able to achieve anything like that. Would I even want to?

That evening, after we'd finished feeding plastic poles through the tiny holes of the tent fabric, and we'd set up our sleeping bags, we sat back in our chairs watching the flickering of the flames of the fire. Dan poked the fire now and then with a long wooden stick he'd found. Occasionally, we'd say things to each other like, 'It's nice, this, isn't it?' or, 'It's so quiet,' and the other would murmur or make a general nod in agreement. But mainly we just stared into the flames, saying nothing at all, until the blaze calmed to embers.

I think it was the safety of darkness that encouraged Dan to ask how I was doing. We had more of a doing type relationship rather than a how-are-you-doing type friendship. You know those friendships where you mainly just do activity-based stuff and have a good time, rather than going for coffee and putting the world to rights? Dan and I didn't speak much about feelings, so I was slightly surprised when he asked.

'I'm okay,' I said immediately, before correcting myself. 'Well, not okay. But I'm better now I'm here, I think. Because I'm somewhere else, it doesn't feel as though I'm missing out so much.'

'That's good,' Dan replied.

It was a short response, but I knew he meant it.

After a long pause, he continued, 'It's good that you're starting to have memories and do things outside of when you were in a relationship. You can start to think about who you are outside of it now.'

I thought that was a rather astute thing for him to say considering he hadn't been in a relationship in forever.

'I think this could really be your time,' he continued. 'This could be a good thing for you.'

I needed to hear it. 'Thanks, Dan.'

The next morning, I was grateful that I'd insisted on a campsite with a 'proper' shower. Sweat and general stickiness aside, the smoke from the campfire had formed a kind of coating on my skin, hair and clothes, and I couldn't wait to scrub it off. The sound of a tent zip in the morning is always optimistic, and I felt happy to be shuffling to the shower block wrapped in several jumpers and multiple layers of socks. I felt grateful not to be carrying the Pride hangover I knew I would have had if I had been back home.

It was a surprise to find the shower water was warm, and I was able to have a proper wash. I noticed that I began to enjoy being in the shower for the first time in ages, really taking my time to feel the water hitting my head, trickling down my face and onto my shoulders. Maybe it was something about being in nature and away from the city that had made me slow down a little. I could hear birdsong outside, and I inhaled deeply, trying to do that thing mental-health influencers say and 'embrace the moment'. I welcomed a sense of relief rather than the looming sense of sickness and dread I had been used to. My thoughts wandered to London Pride. How it had gone, who had been there, whether my friends had noticed I hadn't been, and was unusually quiet on social media. Or maybe they hadn't thought about it at all. I knew there would be many text messages sent that sore heads would soon wake up to regret, but not me. I switched off the shower, feeling pleased that I'd removed myself from it for a while.

I'm not usually one to look at myself in the mirror as I step out of the shower. The bathrooms I'm usually in steam up the mirrors anyway, so I tend to not bother looking. But the washroom at the campsite had open space on either side of the door, which allowed air in from either side. As I stepped out of the shower and onto the cold tiles, reaching for my towel and balancing so as not to slip, I noticed the reflection of my shape. I was shocked to notice how thin I'd become. I could see the outline of my ribs rippling beneath my skin, and my hip bones stuck out to the sides. My arms looked gangly and shapeless. My jaw was the most defined, and even it looked as though it had sunk. I took a moment to take my new self in.

I reached into my toiletry bag and pulled out my pot of Bio-Oil gel. I dipped my forefinger into it and ran the gel across the length of my top-surgery scars, which had only become a part of me three months previously. They were blisteringly red and they burned a little from the hot shower. I took my time massaging it in circular motions across the length of the scars, then onto my nipples, which were now much smaller than they had been before surgery, cut to a more male-like size. The nipples had healed, and dry skin would begin to creep over them like broken glass if I didn't take care of them properly. I studied myself, trying to familiarize myself with the person looking back at me. I felt unfamiliar even to myself. There was so much of this new body I still had to get used to.

It was an intentionally slow wander back to the tent. I thought about how, in a matter of months (top surgery) and weeks (breakup), my body had changed so dramatically that it had become almost unrecognizable to the person living inside it. I wondered how I hadn't noticed that fat and muscle had fallen from me...to nowhere. I suppose I had been aware that my clothes were a bit looser, but then again, I didn't know what was down to surgery and what was down to heartbreak... or what was down to just refusing to wear anything other than loose T-shirts and trackie bottoms. I thought about the cleverness of the body. Of its ability to reinvent itself, and of how maybe it's a kind of magic that we can change and alter our form. I mused that if our bodies had the power to change themselves so quickly, so drastically, then maybe the mind could too. Maybe one day, hopefully soon, I'd be able to look at myself and feel happy – no longer full of hurt and heartbreak, but content. I clung on to this idea as I went to meet Dan, who had started barbecuing sausages for breakfast.

It turned out that our camping weekend was integral for reflection. I hadn't intended it to be. I just thought it would be an opportunity to escape the drumming of the city during Pride celebrations and visit somewhere neither Dan nor I had been before. But there was something about being in a new place, far away from any memories of Lucy, that was refreshing and cathartic. My body started to loosen a little, my shoulders became less hunched and penned in. I felt like I'd found oxygen again and my lungs were able to expand. It was at this time the relief started to trickle in – a sense that even though things were hard and I was hurting, there might be an opportunity here. A glimmer of hope. Something that resembled a way through. Even though something was immediately devastating...maybe, I thought, this would allow something good to grow. Lucy had broken up with me, not only to allow herself to follow her own path, but because she knew that I needed that too. And so I needed to allow myself the chance to experience being gay, just as Lucy did. I needed to embrace this opportunity and my own calling. After all, I had spent all my adult life with Lucy. I'd been to all my appointments with gender specialists and physically transitioned when with her; I'd recovered from my recent top surgery with her by my side. I hadn't known what it was to be an adult man outside of a relationship. I didn't know what it meant just to be a man at all, having never experienced a boyhood. I wondered if maybe there was something missing...a sense of self away from who and what I was to others. I was a brother, a son, a lover, a nephew, a grandson, a colleague, a neighbour, a friend, God knows, maybe even someone's enemy...but who was I outside of all that? And what or who could I be in the future?

* * *

I'd kind of just assumed, having been with Lucy for five years, that we'd settle down somewhere, maybe change jobs a few times, go on holidays, maybe have kids – although the conversation always ended there because it felt difficult and complicated and far too early for us to be discussing children. But now none of that was on the cards, and the cloudy haze of the breakup began to lift, I started to feel openness and opportunity. I could imagine and think about what life could be like without all these assumptions about a future – maybe I would find someone, maybe I wouldn't, maybe I'd get married, or maybe I wouldn't, maybe I'd be in an open relationship... I just didn't know.

I learned that there is power in not knowing and just being able to figure it out as you go along, rather than being so long-sighted that you miss everything else – all the other opportunities that present themselves along the way. Despite the hurt and the pain and feeling like I'd never be the same ever again...maybe I didn't want to be. Maybe this was my chance. The blinkers had been lifted, and maybe being broken up with was a gift. Like I'd been given agency to pursue my own life in whatever way I wanted to. I guess that's the best bit about being gay or queer, isn't it? We get to dictate our own life and the ways in which we want it to play out, rather than being marked by if we have or haven't got a partner, or if we have or haven't got married, or if we have or haven't got children. And for that, I realized, I was pleased to have a chance to start over again, but better and more myself this time.

* * *

I was way too late in realizing, having never really gone through a heartbreak like that before, that what I really needed was Elton John. The first step on the road to recovery is – no, not acceptance or even anger – it's Elton. A bit of pop-rock-ALL-frills-attached-with-extra-large-sunglasses-and-maybe-a-Donald-Duck-outfit-for-the-Central-Park-Concert-(Google it)-bit-of-lose-yourself-in-dance campery. This was around the time that the new *Rocket Man* movie came out, and to say I became obsessed would be an understatement. Tube journey – Elton. Morning shower – Elton. Getting stains out of the God-knows-how-old living room rug – Elton. His music and performances on YouTube became the soundtrack to my life. So much so that the downstairs neighbour knocked rather hurriedly on the door of my flat to say that while she, too, loved *Saturday Night's Alright for Fighting*, it was a Wednesday, not as good the thirteenth time round and could I possibly turn it down, or better – off. Why anyone would want to miss out on such a banger was beyond me, but not being one for confrontation, I reluctantly obliged. Instead, I put my headphones in, side-stepping, hip-wriggling and shoulder-shrugging my way around my bedroom. If you're in need of a visual aid, consider Hugh Grant in *Love Actually*. I don't think my dancing was much better for my neighbour, because after a rather rigorous foot shuffle, which left me out of breath and embarrassingly red-faced, a note reading 'PLEASE stop banging around!!' had been shoved under the front door.

Elton John taught me three things:

1. Elton's raucous dress style and costumes taught me that it's okay to express yourself however you like. You don't have to be limited to what others think you *should* wear.

2. It's possible to go through some really difficult times (in Elton's case, drug addiction and not being out as gay publicly for a long time, amongst other things) and still come out the other side *still standin'* (yeah, yeah, yeah).

3. You really can burn off a lot of energy and anger dancing around your bedroom.

Elton's music (and my poor dancing) helped take the edge off the breakup and helped me find a way to channel my anger. It was a distraction, I suppose. I could block out all my own intruding and self-deprecating thoughts via beats in my headphones. Thoughts like: was it all my fault? What if I wasn't gay; could I not just ignore these feelings? What if I'd never transitioned to male in the first place? Maybe then she'd still fancy me and we'd still be together.

All the dancing and energy in the music kept my anxiety and messy, confusing thoughts at bay by pumping so much adrenaline and endorphins through my body that by the end I started to get hungry and tired again. After months of losing weight, of it shredding from my body to seemingly nowhere, and not being able to sleep, this was a welcome return. I suppose some people get over breakups by going for long runs, hooking up with strangers or hitting the weights in the gym. For me, it was Elton and *terrible* dancing.

I didn't consider this at the time, but on reflection I think it was important I reached for a gay artist to help me through. To help bridge the gap between being a trans man with a girlfriend to beginning to understand my own gayness. Now, I'm not one for walking down Clapham Common in neon-green feather wings, sequinned baseball kit or bulging flares like Elton, but it was the confidence that gave me hope. On one of my many late-night internet travels watching old Elton music videos and interviews, I read a *Variety* article in which Elton had been quoted as saying, 'It's wonderful to be gay. I love being gay. I really do. And I think I wouldn't have had the life I've had if I hadn't been gay. I'm very proud of that.'[1] I wondered if I, too, might be able to reach a point where I could be comfortable being gay. Happy, proud – perhaps even glad. Maybe I could forgive myself for being gay and for the fact that it was one of the reasons why my relationship with Lucy had ended. Given the fact that I had been in a heterosexual relationship for the majority of my adult life and I'd never so much as dipped my toe into a gay male world, that gladness and forgiveness seemed like a long way off. I just had to figure out where to start.

---

1   Malkin, M. (2019) 'Elton John Has a Message for Struggling LGBTQ Youth: "Be Proud of Who You Are".' *Variety*, 20 June, 2019. Accessed on 17/08/2022 at https://variety.com/2019/music/features/elton-john-on-being-gay-1203248152

The Lesbian to Straight Man to Gay Man Timeline

I t took approximately ten years to complete the lesbian to straight man to gay man timeline. Age 13 to 23 – ten years! And I didn't even get a certificate for it. If I had, my dad might have handed me a fiver as he used to when I got a certificate for something as a kid. Like a 'Yeah! You swam 500 metres' or 'You're most improved player' or the 'We see you've tried really hard at maths but you're not quite there yet' award. They don't do 'New name, new you' or 'Congratulations on getting your tits lobbed off' cards in The Card Factory, but they really should.

It's probably worth explaining how I went from thinking I was a straight girl to being a gay man because 1) context is important and 2) it's always the part people find most interesting about my transition when they've had a few beers at the pub. And they're right; it is interesting. So here goes.

As I mentioned in my author note, some LGB people and trans-exclusionary radical feminists (TERFs) believe that transitioning is a form of conversion therapy. These people believe that in the case of trans men, young 'tomboys' are shamed so much for being 'different', and the misogynistic pressure on women is so heavy and burdensome, that these young girls (as they call them) transition to be boys. They say that many of these young 'tomboys' may have grown up to understand themselves as lesbians and would have been embraced by the lesbian community later in their life. They would have come to understand that their masculinity is accepted, embraced even, in the lesbian community and they would have come to realize that they did not have to change their gender. In short, they say that if I had embraced my masculinity and tomboyish behaviour as a kid, then I would have understood that I can be masculine and a girl at the same time and I wouldn't have transitioned; I'd have (probably) grown up to be lesbian. Where this falls down (and quite quickly, I might add) is that transness runs way deeper than this rather flimsy notion of gender and that I've pretty much always fancied men.

As part of the LGB Alliance's End Conversion Therapy campaign, they started the hashtag #StopTransingTheGay-Away.[1] This provoked a flurry of angry tweets on my own Twitter feed. Tweets like:

@TwitterUser1
Sex is Real! Biology is meaningful. Sexuality is based on a person's sex, not their pronouns. Trans is an intervention, something you do not something you are. #StopTransingTheGayAway[2]

1   LGB Alliance (2022) 'End Conversion Therapy.' Accessed on 17/08/2022 at https://lgballiance.org.uk/end-conversion-therapy
2   @TwitterUser1 7:24 p.m., 13 May 2021.

> **@TwitterUser2**
> EXACTLY! Thank you! No child is 'born in the
> wrong body' no 'girl brain in a boy body'. No.
> Let's support them to mature into healthy bodies.
> #StopTransingTheGayAway #NotBornInTheWrongBody[3]

Now, given the hashtag #StopTransingTheGayAway, you would think that people who have transitioned were one gender and gay, then transitioned, and then were a different gender and heterosexual. For example, they assume that I was once a lesbian girl and have now transitioned to be a straight boy. Transitioning would, in their eyes, make my gay go away.

The issue with this, of course, is that it has not. I'm as gay as they come. In fact, statistically speaking, trans people are *more* likely to be lesbian, gay or bi. In a chapter of *Trans Britain: Our Journey from the Shadows*, Sarah Brown (the only openly transgender elected politician in the UK between 2010 and 2014), found that 'a lot – perhaps as many as half – of trans people are also lesbian, gay or bisexual'.[4] Certainly, in my own experience of meeting new trans people, attending youth groups and being on online support forums, I have found this to be the case too. Perhaps even more than half. So to that end, the hashtag doesn't add up. Transitioning doesn't make gayness go away; in fact, if you're trans, you're even more likely to be gay, lesbian or bi. I have a few theories as to why this might be. Perhaps trans people are more likely to experiment with their sexuality because they

---

3   @TwitterUser2 12:03 a.m., 28 March 2021.
4   Brown, S. (2018) 'The Activist New Wave.' In Christine Burns (ed.) *Trans Britain: Our Journey from the Shadows*. London: Unbound. p.313.

have explored their gender first. Or maybe the genitalia of a potential partner don't matter so much for trans people because they understand that it is not the genitals that make a person, but rather the nature of *who* they are rather than *what* they are. Ultimately, the reason why someone is or isn't gay doesn't really matter. What matters is that trans people are more likely to be LGBQ than the LGB Alliance would like you to think.

Before I move on and share my own lesbian to straight man to gay man timeline and some of my own experience, I feel I need to tackle some of the other language used in the tweets I've just shared. Mainly because I have the opportunity here to set the record straight (trans people are often left out of conversations regarding transition in the media) and it would be insolent and wrong of me to move on without doing so. The first untruth is that trans people don't think sex is real. This is simply not true. I am *very* aware that sex is real because 1) I am very good at it and 2) I wake up every morning to my own vulva. I can feel and touch it. I am aware that it exists as part of my body. That doesn't, however, make me a woman. My genitals do not define my gender any more than my nails define my height.

The second false claim is that we don't believe biology is meaningful. This may be true in the sense that I don't believe that biology equals gender and that it should define a person (after all, we are all so much more than our bodies – trans or not) but it doesn't mean I don't think biology is meaningful. My trans body *is* meaningful. It is what separates me from being a cisgender man. It means I have a difference and a history that is unlike that of cisgender men. I wouldn't be the man I am today if I hadn't lived 18 years of my life as a woman. I'm proud of my difference.

This neatly brings me on to my third point, which is something I actually agree with @TwitterUser2 on – I know, I didn't think I'd say it either! And that is that we are not 'born in the wrong body'. It's true, the line 'born in the wrong body' feels as old as trans history itself. 'I'm born in the wrong body' has historically been used and exhausted by trans people to try to explain the feeling of discomfort and dysphoria in our bodies. Trans healthcare (hormones, surgeries, voice therapy, counselling, etc.) has not been designed by trans people – it's been created by cisgender health professionals – so it's historically been an easier way for trans people to explain to cisgender medical professionals how they feel so they can get access to healthcare. These recognizable, cliché lines became important because medical professionals were gatekeepers, the ones who decided who and who can't receive healthcare and surgery. So by fitting nicely and neatly into recognizable boxes, it is easier to use this sort of phrasing than to try to explain the nuance of gender and identity and risk not receiving any help at all.

I have to say that I've never really resonated with the 'born in the wrong body' thing. There are times (and these times are frequent) when I have burned for a tall body, longed for a straight torso rather than an hourglass figure and dreamt of a flat rather than busty chest. There was a time quite recently where I cried into my McDonald's Big Flavour Wrap all the way home because I felt that a penis was missing from my body...and that my hips fell outside of most men's jeans. I found it distressing. That is my dysphoria and my reality. However, despite pain and longing some of the time, I've never really felt like my body is 'wrong'. My body is mine and it is all I have ever known. There are things I wish I could add to it or take away, but at the same time I cannot help but feel that I was not born in the wrong body but rather the wrong world. A world that teaches us that transness is a synonym for 'broken body' and therefore needs to be fixed. I do not need to be fixed. No trans person needs to be fixed. We are beautiful the way we are – whether we decide that surgery and hormones are the right path for us or not.

You may well be wondering, 'Well why get surgery then, if it's not fixing a problem?' It's a good question, and one I've spent many long, uncomfortable nights arguing with myself about. When I began the process of getting testosterone through an NHS Gender Identity Clinic and started the referral process for top surgery (surgery to remove breasts), I did not pursue this in order to fix myself or for others to view me as fixed. I never viewed myself as a broken body in the first place. Rather, I took hormones and had surgery to become closer to the person I have always been and the person I want to become. It was about finding myself away from distraction. To feel present and closer to myself. For the world to view me as I always have. This does not mean my body is broken. For me, transitioning was more about coming home. It was the biggest act of self-care and self-love I have ever been able to offer myself.

The last point that I disagree with then, is that 'sexuality is based on a person's sex, not their pronouns'. Ask yourself this question: when you see someone you fancy in a bar, a club, a coffee shop, or, I don't know, Tesco, what do you see? Do you see their thick forearm hair? Or their sharp, angular jawline? Or maybe they have a gorgeous curly-on-top, short-back-and-sides haircut? Perhaps after talking to them you notice they have a soft singing voice tha— okay, yes, I'm talking about Olly from *Years and Years*. And no, I haven't met him in Tesco or at a bar, and I don't know what I'd even do if

I did. Anyway, I'm getting distracted. The point is, you don't look at someone's genitals first, do you? That's not the initial attraction. It may be their look, their style, their character, their voice. So basing attraction purely on genitalia when there are so many other things that make a person makes little sense.

From lesbian...

Now, shock horror, I never really was a lesbian. I know, a bit of a miss-sell on the chapter title – sue me. The reason why sometimes I feel like I know a bit about the lesbian world and occasionally affectionately refer to my 'lesbian days' is that there was a time when I genuinely thought I was a lesbian. I tried really, really, *really* hard to be a gay girl. I figured that with everyone already thinking I was a lesbian – my classmates, teachers, parents of my friends, maybe even my own parents (I don't know; I've never asked them), maybe I *was* a lesbian but I just hadn't started to fancy women yet. I assume they thought I was a lesbian because I fitted all those stereotypes – you know, the ones about lesbians having long hair tied back into a low ponytail, liking 'masculine' sports, wearing boyish plaid shirts and trousers (never skirts – and if they are camo, that's a bonus). I'm well aware these are hideous stereotypes, and not every lesbian or tomboy is like this, but unfortunately, I was a walking cliché. I know, I know. Fancying women and being a woman are pretty much the *only* criteria for being a lesbian. I think I thought that I'd just grow into it or something. That I might eventually realize that those people were right. And I guess I did like girls a bit...I think...but not as much as I liked boys. I really, *really* liked boys. I liked their long torsos, flat chests, Adam's apples, deep voices and short, messy, bed-head hair. All the things I liked about them I also wanted for myself. So there was something about the word 'lesbian' that never gelled with me. It didn't sit right because that meant I was a girl liking girls...both of which I *knew* weren't true.

*   *   *

I remember being at high school one day. My knees felt like shrapnel as I entered the locker room, letting my feet drag behind me. It was a blisteringly cold day outside, and while my shin pads had protected my lower legs from becoming scratched and bruised during PE, my knees hadn't been so lucky. They were crimson. We raised our hockey sticks, launching them into the wooden box at the end of the bench, before heading to our own lockers to get changed from our mud-ridden and stinking PE kits. I was always the last to change from my sports kit into my school uniform, taking my time to dillydally and dodge the squirts of Impulse Instant Crush body spray, which seemed to be that year's 'thing'. I sat on the bench for a while, head bowed, and tapped the floor with my studded hockey boots. I liked the sound they made as the metal touched against the tiled floor. I liked, too, the feel of the boots on my feet over my long nylon sports socks. We'd only recently been able to wear studded boots, a delicacy usually reserved for the boys, but in some lucky win, we'd been allowed to share the same grass sports pitch and got to wear 'proper' boots. There was something stronger and more masculine about the studded boots as opposed to the AstroTurf plastic trainers we used to wear. The Astro boots felt pretend, like we weren't trusted, or we were too delicate for the metal ones. I felt more confident and at home in the proper boots, like they added armour.

It felt unfair that the boots had to be the first thing I had to take off, which meant I lost not only a half an inch of height but also several inches of confidence too. That's why I waited as long as I could to change back into my knee-length school skirt and almost-see-through ten-denier tights. I wanted to stay in my masculine, mud-smeared boots for as long as possible.

'Are you pervin' on us?!'

Fuck. It was Andrea, the ringleader of the school netball team. The general, with her brigade of posh and immaculately turned-out teammates, looking at me as though they were stone-washed emperors.

'No, I'm not pervin' on you. I'm just gettin' changed.' I could feel the heat rising within me.

'Why yeh just sat there watchin' then, if you're not pervin' on us?'

'Cus I'm jus—'

'Miss! Miss! She's pervin' on us. Like lookin' and stuff! She's not even changed yet!'

Miss Brighton, our PE teacher and one of the most patient and supportive teachers I knew, knocked on the locker room door. She, herself – with her short, dark buzz cut and frequent advocacy for trying to get football and tag rugby in the girl's curriculum – was long rumoured to be a lesbian, but she always kept details of her home life to herself. She studied the lengths of us, her eyes flitting to me, to them and back to me again.

'Just get changed, girls.'

The bell rang and the netball girls hurried off to their class, brushing against me as they left, leaving me to get changed in a hurry and alone.

Later that day, I stood outside the school gates waiting for a lift from my mum. She had a multi-stop trip, finishing work at the college she used to teach at, picking my brother up from his school the other side of town and then coming to collect me. I waited at the gates most evenings, nervously looking at the time on my Motorola flip phone, hoping they hadn't been in some terrible car accident or forgotten me. They never did; the traffic was just always bad.

I looked through the cars on the congested main road and searched for my mum's number plate. Without warning, Andrea and her mate Becca came into view. They were tall, which made them key players on the netball team. I, being the smallest in my year, played centre – light on my feet and speedy.

I stood with my back against the painted metal railings as they approached.

'We know you're a lesbian, just admit it,' Andrea said. Her eyes hardened.

'Am not a lesbian. I don't know what you're talkin' about,' I replied, more confidently now I was outside the school gates and in full view of traffic.

'C'mon, just admit it! We won't tell anyone.'

'I'm not a lesbian,' I repeated, firmer and more defiant this time.

'We just want to know, like, why do you like girls? Who do you fancy? We heard it was Jess.'

'I don't.'

They got closer, towering over me, and my neck strained in order to see Andrea's face. I could feel the skin around my throat tighten where my Adam's apple should be. It felt nice.

Andrea glared at me. I wondered what she might do next. She couldn't hit me; we were in full view of traffic, and plus, she'd likely get suspended or kicked off the netball team. Her eyes held my gaze.

She didn't blink and neither did I.

Eventually, when the tension proved too much, she pulled away and walked with Becca in the direction of the city centre.

I stepped away from the railing and took a deep breath. It felt like a lucky escape. I hadn't backed down – that was the main thing – and I felt proud of myself for standing my ground. But at the same time, I felt a sense of shame and confusion. I wasn't lying. I didn't think I was a lesbian, but surely there was something they saw in me that told them I was. What was it? What did they see in me that I had clearly missed in myself? And, say I was a lesbian, and I finally managed to realize it... Would this be the life I would lead? Being almost pinned against metal railings and quizzed about my sexuality by my peers wasn't really something I had envisioned for my life. I felt shame. Shame that I hadn't backed myself more. Shame that I was potentially hiding something from myself. Shame that I was denying I was a lesbian because it felt like I was letting down friends of mine who I knew were gay. I wonder if those girls ever felt shame about interrogating me or if it's stuck with them since. Somehow, I don't think so.

Not long later, someone in a white Mercedes wound the blacked-out passenger-side window down and threw a lit fag end on the pavement next to me. I scowled and went to stub it out with my shoe. (I'd watched enough episodes of *EastEnders* to know that lit cigarette ends are dangerous – that episode where Dot Branning falls asleep and a cigarette lands in a paper bin and catches fire, burning down the whole Branning house, is not easily forgotten).

It took a few seconds before I realized that it wasn't actually a cigarette butt but rather a small firework, which had, presumably, been aimed directly at me with a misjudged landing. I turned on my heel and ran as far as I could up the patchwork pavement before loud bangs and smoke emerged and sparks flew in the air. My eyes darted to see where the Mercedes had gone, and to maybe catch the number plate, but it had sped off. The firework continued to spit white flashes over the pavement before burning into a slump, smoke still escaping from the end.

Luckily, none of the sparks touched me. But I was left shaken. Despite there being many onlookers in cars, nobody came to help or check that I was okay, which was somehow even worse than the firework being thrown itself. It was like I was invisible. Or maybe it was that I was visible but nobody around cared. Somehow, that felt worse.

I don't know whether it was those girls in that car or whether it was a complete coincidence. I'd like to think that it was the latter and that it wasn't punishment for not 'admitting' that I was gay. In either case, I blamed myself. What if I hadn't stood there? Would they have done that if I were a boy? Did it happen because I'd denied I was a lesbian? Was it, in some way, a punishment from the universe for being different? Or was it just a coincidence? I wondered whether I should report it to the police or my school. But that might mean relaying the conversation beforehand about maybe being a lesbian and I couldn't share that – not with anyone. That would be far too shameful and I wasn't ready for those types of conversations yet.

My mum arrived some ten minutes later, apologizing for

the traffic being hideously bad. 'Get in, love. Sorry about the traffic. Are you alright? You look a bit pale. Do you not feel well?'

'No, Mum. I'm fine,' I replied. I faked a smile, which my mum knew better than to believe.

I spent the hour car journey home quiet but fidgety. I replayed what had happened in my head and tried not to think about what the next day might look like back at school.

I can only assume that my masculinity was the one thing that made them think I was a lesbian. I was stereotyped and then bullied before I'd even had the chance to figure out my gender and sexuality for myself. I find the idea of gender presentation alluding to a sexual orientation interesting because some people may think that gender and sexuality are completely separate things – your sexuality is who you fancy, and your gender is who you are as a person. I understand this in theory. However, in my life, with my flirting with genders and sexualities, I've found these two core facets to be interwoven and inseparable. It was my gender presentation – my masculinity – that made them assume my sexuality, not who I was dating or what sexual or romantic acts I was or wasn't performing. To that end, gender (and our performance of it in the world) must play some role in our understanding of sexuality. Right? Trying to describe one without the other is near impossible.

As a kid, growing up as a tomboy was mostly...fine. Sure, it might have been a bit unusual and my parents probably wished I didn't scream at the prospect of wearing pink knickers or decapitate the Barbie dolls my Aunt got me for my birthday, but hey. My parents thought that I was adventurous and sporty, which they mostly encouraged. I suppose they were comforted by the fact that society tells them you'll just grow out of tomboyishness when puberty hits and boys come on the scene. My parents did take me, if a little hesitantly, to girls' only football teams and surprised me with a trip to the Manchester United football shop during the summer holidays one year. Being boyish as a kid – fine. Being a masculine young woman throughout and after puberty – unacceptable.

It seemed at times as if everyone around me thought I was a lesbian, and I received homophobic bullying as a result. I found this difficult and confusing, not only because many things are when you're growing up, but because it wasn't true. Sure, I did try to go out with girls, but I didn't feel like that made me a lesbian. You have to be a girl to be a lesbian, and even then, in my very core, I knew I wasn't a girl. Then, I'm pretty sure another criterion for being a lesbian is solely liking women. Which was also not true. Boys were my kryptonite. My nectar. The people I daydreamed of as I went to sleep and my first thought in the morning. Those were the people who got me giddy and excited, and I'd take hours getting dressed to impress them. So even though I tried really hard to be lesbian, and tried to fit myself into the box that was imposed and projected onto me without my permission, it didn't work. I never really felt it. Truthfully, my lesbian days mainly just consisted of messages to girl pals on MSN Messenger like:

> hey... so umm... keep this a secret...

> but

I like you

If they replied positively and expressed interest in me, too, this might be met with a 'wud you like 2 b my gf then?' Before, predictably, avoiding each other in class and school corridors for a week and an inevitable 'I think we shud breakup' a week later. If she replied, 'I don't think of you in that way', I'd usually just send an 'omg wrong person lollll' and forget it ever happened. Fourteen-year-old me thought I was very clever. Mid-twenties me...not so much.

Ultimately, it was my disorientation and confusion around sexuality that led me to think about gender. Anyone who says that gender and sexuality are entirely separate things also needs to think about what it means to be gay, or lesbian, or bi, or pan, or heterosexual. For example, being gay means being one gender and liking the same gender. The definitions of these sexual identities are inherently based on the gender of the person with that identity. As soon as I'd managed to figure that out, it became clear that I had to consider and interrogate my own sense of self first before I could make sense of my own sexuality. For me, this happened in the theatre.

Mum was thrilled when I said I wanted to give musical theatre a go. It was something better – more feminine and joyful – than standing on the side of football pitches in the cold. Maybe she thought the singing and dancing would help me embrace my femininity as I moved closer to puberty. But for me, the theatre had nothing to do with any of that. The theatre was a happy place. A place that was, when the curtains opened and lights flooded the stage, a world of unknowns. It was a plastic art, where the staging, set, characters and story could be moulded in whatever way we wanted. For me, the theatre offered possibility.

Mum would drop me off at the bottom of Forest Bank Road in the village in Lancashire where I grew up, and I would begin the steep climb up the hill towards the grey brick Methodist church, weaving around on the thin pavement, trying to dodge all the other kids clambering out of cars that were perched scruffily on the double yellows. Rakefoot was one of those parochial church halls you get in small villages. The type where the 'dressing room' is actually the chapel – where powder, lipsticks and tights adorn the fold-up tables and questionable wigs and obscenely filled bras hang next to wooden sculptures of Jesus. And it was inevitable that during the interval, someone's gran would stride down the aisle, daring well-meaning parents to buy *another* strip of raffle tickets for a chance to win some half-arsed wine. In the winter, we'd all have to wear thick coats for rehearsals, huddling around the electric heater for warmth, seeing our breath escape from our mouths as we sang.

I was never under the illusion that I was any good. And thank God, because I don't think I'm really cut out for audition rejections and being at the mercy of an audience eight times a week. I could just about act (on a good day), I could barely dance, and, well, I couldn't find a tune if it tracked me down and grabbed me by the ankles. Thankfully for me and our audience, amateur theatre isn't really about being good or not – it's about wallflowers being together and finding each other. Although, I really should apologize to the audiences that had to endure my wailing... Take this as my official 'I'm sorry'.

On a familiarly damp and dreary Saturday afternoon when I was 14, I walked through the doors of Rakefoot, greeted by the same friendly faces I saw each week. Jess was there, as was Sam, Sammy, Austen, Tom, Clare... They were all there for the same reason I was – because they loved the theatre and it was a welcome escape from the harshness of school life.

As with any local amateur-dramatic lessons, there was a sixteen-to-one ratio of girls to boys. This suited me just fine because it meant there were always of plenty of decent male parts available. This week we were rehearsing for *Oliver!* Given my...let's call it limited...theatrical ability, I had auditioned for the part of Mr Sowerberry, the undertaker who Oliver visits when he first runs away from the workhouse. I'm not really sure that's what my mum had in mind when she took me to musical theatre lessons but, bless her, she went with it.

Sally, our head of costume (the only member of the costume 'department', in fact) handed me a yellow plastic hanger, on which hung a pair of pressed black trousers and a co-ordinating tailcoat (button missing), one men's white shirt, a black tie (matte) and one of those thin-plastic-but-looks-like-fabric top hats. Sally raised her arm and signalled for me to go to try the costume on in the toilets at the back of the hall.

I started taking my clothes off in the loo, folding them neatly on top of the closed toilet seat. I was naked except for pink knickers, matching socks and a grey sports bra – supporting more than its fair share of boobage. I glanced briefly in the mirror behind the door before reaching for the hanger, now perched precariously on the edge of the hand dryer. I took the hanger and removed the pressed trousers carefully before stepping into them. Immediately I noticed how they were much thicker and more rigid than my own. As I pulled the fabric up around my thighs, then bum, then waist, I was increasingly aware that the material was unforgiving and didn't seem to want to bend and mould around my body – not in the same way women's trousers did. They wanted to stand firm and shapeless. I noticed how much tighter everything felt and I purposely left the top trouser button undone while reaching for the white shirt in the hope that those two minutes it took me to finish getting dressed might make all the difference and my hips might miraculously be able to fit comfortably.

Pulling my arms through the sleeves of the shirt felt easy enough, but I noticed how much stiffer the collar felt around my neck in comparison to those of the blouses I wore for school. Rather than the collar lying flat around my collar bones with a tiny lapel, the collar now rose to the top of my neck, stopping just short of my chin. I tucked the bottom of my shirt into my trousers, the excess fabric bunching and crumpling inside.

A knock on the door. Sally was in a hurry to get through the costumes for the whole cast and, as she reminded me through the door, she had Mr Bumble, Nancy and 40 Victorian orphans still to dress.

'Are you ready to come out?'

'Yeah, nearly!'

I pulled the trousers up slightly above my hips and buttoned them (just about) with the help of an inside clasp – another male-only trouser feature and another first for me. (Why is it only the men who get large pockets, thick, quality fabrics and inside clasps?!) I hurriedly opened the toilet door, the fabric at the bottom of my trousers dragging underneath my pink flowery socks.

'Very smart. Now we just need to turn those up at the

bottom, and maybe fold over the wrists of your shirt so they're not too long... There. Much better. And the jacket?'

I fumbled behind me for the jacket while Sally pricked the bottom of my trousers with a needle.

'There we go. Much better!'

I did feel much better. The jacket hid my curvy waist, which had been bulging out the sides of my shirt giving me an unwanted muffin-top. It gave me a flatter, straighter profile. The jacket, too, hid my arse, which I swore would almost rip if I tried to sit down. Thankfully, as an undertaker, my performance was more of a slow shuffle than high-kick razzle-dazzle, so I was about 70 per cent certain there wouldn't be a split-hem trouser situation mid-funeral procession.

I went back into the toilet and started to tie the black tie the same way my dad had taught my brother when he'd first started high school. I'd never worn a tie before, but somehow, I realized, I'd remembered each step.

I stood back and watched the mirror like a laptop screen. My eyes searched my reflection closely. From my head, with a black-bobbled ponytail parked at the base of my neck, down to broader looking shoulders, the jacket arms coming right down to my knuckles, to the thick white collar with neatly tied tie falling over my breasts, which were clamped down as much as possible by my sports bra. My eyes moved to where my trousers sat on my waist – much lower than I was used to – and I could feel the sweaty, shiny fabric sticking to the insides of my thighs where my boxers should have been. I remembered I was wearing pink knickers and suddenly felt quite embarrassed, my face hotting up a little. It was the contrast as much as anything. It felt silly, pink knickers underneath a men's suit, and I started to feel ashamed. It was like I was missing something... Then my eyes travelled south, down to my thighs and knees, then to the bottom of my trousers, where the pins held fabric that would soon be cut and hemmed to size. I took a step back to try to take it all in.

A rap on the door.

'Have you got changed? I need to get Mr Bumble int—'

'Yeah, I'm coming!'

* * *

Despite some unfamiliarity with the type of clothes I was wearing and the way in which they were shaped around my body, this was the first opportunity I'd ever had to wear a men's suit, or men's clothes at all, really. I was excited – euphoric even – at the prospect, and for the first time I'd seen myself in clothes that I'd always aspired to wear but was never allowed to. Growing up, girls' clothes were good. Boys' clothes were bad. I'd always longed to wear a boys' school uniform, complete with grey school trousers, white shirt and tie tied ludicrously short. The boys who got to wear those uniforms didn't realize how lucky they were, and I was always confused when I'd hear people say, 'Urgh I don't want to wear a suit – they're so uncomfortable.' For me, I could only ever dream of wearing one.

Wearing very traditional gendered clothing felt like a definitive moment. If playing a male character was the question, the costume fitting was the answer. As I stared back at myself, ignoring my ponytail but noticing how broad my shoulders looked, how square my torso was, how neatly pressed the trousers were...I realized these were the clothes, and the body, I'd longed for.

I'd always kind of imagined that when you wore clothes

the right size they'd fit perfectly. Having only worn women's clothes previously, I knew that of course they catered for bigger hips, shorter bodies and boobs. So when I tried on the suit, despite feeling elated and affirmed that these were the type of clothes I'd longed for, I realized that they didn't quite fit in the way I'd anticipated they would, or in the way I would have liked. What became clear, apart from the differences in clothing semantics like buttons, lapels and zips, was how they sat on my body. These clothes were designed for cis men's bodies – a straight up and down, tall, box-like figure with wide shoulders and a narrow waist. In contrast, I was short and curvy, with large, protruding breasts that weren't successfully hidden by a suit jacket or tie – no matter how hard I tried to crush them down with my sports bra. It was conflicting. I was wearing the clothes I wanted to, finally (although it must be said that I didn't quite dream it would be a funeral suit, but nonetheless), but the fit reminded me that these clothes weren't designed for bodies like mine. Suits are designed for cisgender men's bodies. Skirts and dresses are designed for cisgender women's bodies. There weren't, and still aren't, any clothes designed specifically for trans bodies. So the suit felt too tight and too loose in all the wrong places. It was a difficult and overwhelming realization to come to in that moment, because I realized that the body I desperately wanted – that of a cis man – I would never fully have.

If playing male roles in the theatre was my baptism into maleness, then playing Mr Sowerberry was my confirmation. While I'd worn women's blouses and trousers that alluded to a male role before, this was my first time wearing actual men's clothing. The theatre allowed me to play and explore characters, roles, costumes and dynamics that I wouldn't have been able to on the other side of the stage. I know it isn't quite an 'I am what I am' moment, but it gave me space to think about what I liked, what clothes I felt comfortable in, how we can shift and perform gender. The experience of embodying and projecting maleness in a performance, and that being seen and responded to by the cast and audience, felt incredibly important and validating. I was viewed for the first time as how I felt inside. I could believe, even for the briefest of moments, that I was male – my performance, my character, my clothing wholly and unquestionably male. Walking from the wings felt like respite from an otherwise female existence, which always felt like trying to fit a square peg into a circular hole. I suspect I was probably the happiest anyone has ever been while wearing a funeral suit, and I was sad when the production finally came to an end.

To straight man...

Much has been written about hypermasculinity – or performative/toxic masculinity, as you may know it – and the harm it does. In essence, hypermasculinity is the belief that in order to be a man, you must in no way resemble a woman. *Especially* when it comes to strength, looks, aggression and sexuality. Masculinity, some believe, is about toughness, antifemininity and power. We often – but not often enough – hear about the way in which this affects women. How men can be misogynistic, entitled, harmful, abusive, objectifying, cruel and neglectful (this list is not exhaustive) towards women. The truth of the matter is that it doesn't stop there. Hypermasculinity is harmful towards everyone – men, women and all genders. It is a plague that must be addressed.

For example, gay men write about how their attraction to

other men and any hint of femininity or campness may make them a target for bullying and abuse. It's no coincidence that fathers telling their sons to 'not be so soft' is a way of telling them that gentleness is not to be tolerated. A boy/man must be hard, be rough, be firm and stand his ground. Or perhaps your peers have said to you, 'You got beaten by a girl', which roughly translates to 'You are less than a man.' Straight men, too, recognize the oppression and restraints hypermasculinity brings. It has been a slow process, but recently more men have started to open up about the heavy weight of masculinity and the expectations placed on them by parents, their peers, society and themselves. To give only a few examples as to how this might play out in everyday life, men can sometimes feel like 'self-care is for women' and therefore won't take the time to take care of their health – including making appointments to go see a doctor or a dentist. It might present itself as stigma about getting treatment for mental health conditions in fear of it being seen as weakness and therefore threatening their sense of masculinity.

When I started to physically transition and take testosterone, it changed my appearance. My voice changed first, breaking about three months in. Then came the fat redistribution, receding hairline, thickening of skin, increased body hair and development of facial fuzz. I felt stronger within myself and found I had much more energy than I did before. I was ready for all of this. I read it all online, and I'd seen videos on YouTube of people physically transitioning before I did. But what I was not ready for was how hypermasculinity, and perceived hypermasculinity, would put pressure on me and seem to appear out of nowhere once society started to read me as male on the street.

I first became aware of this when I was walking from my

flat to a lecture at uni. It was a nice morning, late spring I think, and I was wearing a plain T-shirt and long cargo shorts that stopped just below my knees. I know, I know, cargo pants...forgive me. I hadn't yet found men's fashion, never mind the fashion of gay men! Anyway, I was walking down the pavement and I spotted a woman walking towards me in the opposite direction. She was carrying heavy Sainsbury's bags in both hands. When we reached almost a metre away from each other, I noticed how she instinctively moved to the side to let me pass without me having to move. It was a polite and kind thing to do, especially as she was carrying heavy bags, and I felt bad. I also felt like it was unfamiliar. Maybe I just hadn't noticed people moving out of their way for me before, or maybe that morning I was just more in tune and aware of myself, but it felt new, and it felt wrong. It was as if my perceived white masculinity/maleness automatically entitled me to go about my day without moving aside for other people, even if they were more in need of the space. I decided to test the theory. Multiple times over the course of the next few weeks, whenever I found myself walking alone and there was someone walking towards me in the opposite direction, I would test either 1) who moved out of the way first to try to make more room for the other person or 2) how long I could bear to hold my walk before one of us decided to step aside.

The results were not surprising. More often than not, women would instinctively move to the side to make room for me, a man. Most of the time, it was when they were several metres ahead, showing they were quite aware of their surroundings and their place within them. Men, on the other hand, would more often than not simply not move and prefer to barge past without getting out of the way at all. Obviously,

I'm making huge generalizations, and not every woman will move out of the way, and not every man will stand firm in some sort of pavement masculinity contest, but these are the general trends I found. Try it. Or next time you're people watching, just look at the instincts of people and how they move. It can be quite eye opening. As a general rule, I found that women were much more aware of themselves and their surroundings than men.

I found this interesting because I was starting to recognize and benefit from first-hand male privilege – something I'd been aware of from a theoretical point of view but hadn't experienced before. When my voice changed and I went to seminars, I found that with a deeper voice in a male range, people of all genders were more likely to be quiet, listen and appreciate what I was saying than when I had a higher voice in a female range. These are small but significant examples of how male privilege plays out in our day to day.

As a trans man, I found hypermasculinity suffocating. The more I was being recognized as male, the more I felt like I had to conform to traditional ideas of masculinity and misogyny, which I am completely oppose to. Taxi drivers would ask me if I'd 'watched the game', and I'd have to awkwardly feign some football knowledge I had gathered from listening to the radio earlier. Driving instructors would talk about girlfriends and point at women on the street, asking if I'd 'bang them'. Personal trainers at the gym, when I'd actually plucked up the courage to go, would ask if I was going to 'build some muscle for my missus'. It was truly gross.

If hypermasculinity is the belief that in order to be a man a man must in no way resemble a woman, then it follows that being a trans man is pretty tough. I have grown up with an experience of femaleness and femininity for the first

18 years of my life. It took a while to embrace this and see my softness and knowledge of gender and misogyny to be a strength rather than a weakness, and to respect and support the incredible women in my life. I felt, as I was beginning to enter LGBTQ+ support and friendship circles, that I was able to escape a lot of the harshness of hypermasculinity and trying to fit in with the 'lads', but I admit that I really struggled with the sexuality part. I felt like dating women and 'acting as a man' would give me a sense of gender actuality. Like having a girlfriend, and being a boyfriend, would affirm my gender and make me a 'proper man'. The little things, like buying dinner, waiting for her to do her make-up, holding open the door, putting my arm around her shoulder. These were all things symbolic of masculinity and maleness for me. And so that's what I sought, even though I knew from way back in my childhood that my true romantic longing was towards men.

When I found Lucy, at a freshers' barbecue in our first few days at university, it wasn't only her long, red hair, long nails and femininity that caught my attention. It was her sharp wit, charm and fierce intelligence that spoke to me more than anything. After that, her gender hardly mattered at all as a reason why I would or wouldn't want to date her. We connected pretty much on humour alone. And so our relationship grew and blossomed. Although from the outside we might have been seen as a straight couple – a boy and a girl – that's not how we saw it. In fact, when we went to a post-Pride celebration in Soho after marching with an LGBTQ+ charity, we were asked why, if we were straight, were we there. We knew we were in a queer relationship. We both thought of ourselves as bisexual then and therefore our relationship was queer, even if to the outside world we appeared 'straight'. In truth, Lucy and I thought about our sexuality a lot and not at all. We both knew we were queer some ways – I liked men, and Lucy liked some women – even if we didn't act on it. And the sex we had, with dildos, vibrators and strap-ons, felt anything but straight. So we settled on queer, even if that's not how the outside world saw us. Inevitably, I think this disconnect between the queerness we felt of ourselves and how our relationship was recognized by the outside world and other LGBTQ+ people became a bit of a sticking point. It was like we weren't being *seen*. And so, well, you already know the rest.

To gay man

After our breakup, things, understandably, were pretty shit. Everything felt so uncertain – and I'm not one for uncertainty. I'm a man who likes to know what's happening, and I'm known for my colour-coded spreadsheet schedules, even for the smallest of plans. But there are moments in life that you can't really plan for, and the course of your life trajectory changes forever. Like when you're made redundant, or someone close to you passes away, or you're plunged into a lockdown because of Covid-19, or a friend moves to another city, or when you find a lover, or, in my case, lose one. It feels disorientating because the shape of your life has now changed so dramatically, and in such a short space of time, that it's very unsettling and isolating. And because often you're the only one going through these changes (with the exception of pandemic-related lockdowns), it can be exceptionally lonely. It feels as though you need to just carry on as if everything is normal, when life is anything but.

My breakup with Lucy gave me a lot of questions to

think about and address. Questions that I'd successfully avoided up to that point but now had no option but to face. Questions like:

Will anyone want to be in a relationship with me again?

How do I be single (for the first time as an adult)?

Can I love anybody else?

Am I gay or bi? Does that matter?

Will any gay men find me, a trans man, attractive?

Will gay men want to have sex with someone without a penis?

Did my transition and my surgery drive Lucy away?

How do I find gay friends?

What will sex look like now?

How do gay men find each other and date?

Will my family accept me being both gay and trans? Will they understand?

Where do gay guys hang out?

Will I fit into the gay community? Will they accept or reject me?

Will I lose my friends as part of my breakup?

Can I cope with being alone?

Am I attractive enough?

What dating apps do gay men use?

What are poppers? And jockstraps? And twinks/twunks/bears/otters? And PrEP? And saunas? And private Twitter accounts?

How can I be a man when I never had a boyhood?

How do I be open about my transness to potential partners?

How do I react when someone says they've never had sex with someone with a vagina before and they're nervous?

If, and that's a big if, I ever have sex with a man, how will I look after my sexual health as a trans person? Could I take contraceptives if I am also taking testosterone?

And ultimately... What if we've made a huge mistake and I've just lost the love of my life?

These questions spun round my head like a washing machine on a never-ending spin cycle. If I opened the door and started to actually interrogate them, the bubbly water would whoosh out onto the floor like a mini tsunami and flood the place, and I'd be sat on the floor in a sodden mess.

Some of these questions were, I imagine, things that go

through everyone's minds when they've just been dumped. Like if they'll ever find someone again, if they'll lose friends as part of the breakup or if they've just lost the love of their life. But others were more specific to my situation. Stuff like what it meant to be a trans man in a gay world, what sex might look like, where I could find friends and whether I'd be accepted in the gay community. These types of questions were the most isolating because there aren't any cosy breakup movies on Netflix about gay trans men that would comfort me and make me feel better. (I'm thinking a gay trans Bridget Jones – if you're a film producer, let's talk). There weren't any role models I could look up to who were both trans and gay and say to myself, 'Hey, they made it! They're happy. See, it is possible.' I just didn't know what life would now look like, and I found that really tough.

I guess the only way to move forward was to figure it out for myself.

Ready? After you...

Grindr

had predominantly fancied men growing up. I know, I'd been with Lucy for a long time and I undoubtedly loved her, but it seems that was more of a one-off rather than a theme. For the majority of my life so far, I have fancied boys. As a teenager, I paid particular attention to arm hair, veins popping out of muscles – especially on forearms – and took great satisfaction in noticing running shorts that stopped at the perfect height between the knee and the upper thigh. Approximately 15 centimetres, if we're counting. There was something so ethereal yet strong about hairy legs and arms, which captured me. I'd find myself daydreaming far too long and far too often for it to be appropriate. I'd imagine what it would feel like to have my hands running over their legs and what they would smell like. It was something particular to men's hair too, the brittle coarseness and thickness of each hair that joined to make a tapestry on each leg. It ignited something within me. I suppose most of us have things like that, don't we? The very specific aspects of people that we find attractive – the way someone's hair falls, or their arm hair, or their smile, or the dimples in their cheeks. When I was thinking about boys, which was often, I'd find it difficult to stop my mind wandering southwards, and imagine a bulge imprisoned within their pants. I thought of it protruding from underneath their belt buckles and wondered what lay beneath. I longed to see, taste and feel their soft shaft in my hands – and yet, I simultaneously longed for it to be mine. To have my own bulge. To look down and see the protruding roundness of my own limp cock and balls packaged perfectly in my trousers. It was a yearning for theirs and a longing for my own.

It's no surprise then, that a few weeks post-breakup and being fed up with moping around and feeling miserable, I decided to download Grindr. I'm sure you'll have heard of Grindr – gay, straight, bi, asexual, however you identify – you'll know *that* orange app. It's famed even among non-queer people for its accessibility to men and sex. And accessibility to men and sex was *exactly* what I was after.

Grindr has a simple interface: a grid three rows across, often with pictures of headless torsos alongside usernames such as 'Daddy4Younger', 'MansMan', 'Fun Now', 'Local tall guy', 'Blow me' and 'Masculine Top'. Its interface and logo – an orange mask on a black background – suggests something illicit, underground and exciting. The grids are arranged based on proximity, so those at the top are closest to you (possibly only a few feet away) and those near the bottom are furthest from you. It's a working geostatistical map of homosexual lust, designed for shagging convenience. As a newly single man and newbie to 'the gay scene', it seemed like the right place to start. I could dip my toe in and just close the app if it got too much, all from the safety of my bedroom.

Like caution tape, Grindr has a strict black and orange colour palette, which is as recognizable as the 'budduurrt' sound of its notifications. If the 'budduurrt' goes off in a crowded gay bar, there'll be a number of gay men pulling their phones out of the pockets of their high-waisted jeans to see who may have 'tapped' or messaged them. It's popular. Nearly every single (and often not single) gay man I know has it, so downloading it for the first time felt like a rite of passage. I'd say it was like being in a candy store, except it was more like a meat market, with man after man to choose from and a tab for 'fresh' faces – people who had either downloaded Grindr recently or were new to the area.

Grindr, for me, had been the stuff of myth and legend. I'd known of the app and knew that people used it for hook-ups, for making friends, for networking, for twosomes, three-somes and all-other-kind-of-somes. I'd heard tantalizing tales of impropriety and debauchery – it all sounded thrilling. But I'd also heard terrifying stories of users downloading Grindr specifically to find, attack, drug, rape and sometimes kill gay men. I suppose in theory the risks that come with meeting people online are no greater on Grindr than on Tinder and Bumble, except that LGBTQ+ people face far greater risk of experiencing discrimination, harassment and hate crimes than our cisgender, heterosexual peers. And because Grindr is an app for gay men, it's more likely that perpetrators will turn to using it when looking to attack us. I was nervous then, understandably, about meeting up with people from the app for the first time, knowing as I did about the risks of online dating. But the pull of what may lie ahead was enough to click download. I suppose it's the chance, the an-ticipation, that's the lure for everyone. The chance that maybe something could happen. So I lay on my bed and waited for it to install, thumbing my new username and password into the keypad.

* * *

I.

> Hey

> Hey

> Hey you there?

> [sends dick pic]

> [...and another]

> [......and another]

> [.........and another]

2.

> Hey I just met you, and this is crazy

> But check out my profile, and let me pound you maybe?

3.

> Looking for?

4.

> Hey.

> SooO hot

5.

> You are stunning

> Like

> So

> Hot

> Hi

> > Hey, thanks!

> I'm Tom

> Didn't think I'd find trans attractive before

Enough. I swiped upwards with my forefinger to close the
app and took a long exhale, closing my eyes. I had debated
about whether or not to include my transness on my profile.
On the one hand, I didn't see why I needed to share such a
personal detail about myself with people I'd never met before.
It could be dangerous and attract negative, hurtful comments.

I could have just played it safe and come out as trans if the conversation had been going well. But on the other hand, it felt dishonest. Not dishonest to them – me simply existing isn't being deceitful or lying about who I am – but rather dishonest to myself. Being trans is so much a part of who I am, how I navigate the world and my perspective on things that it felt like ignoring such a rich and important part of myself was self-denial. A rejection of myself. The world rejects trans people enough as it is, so I made a deliberate choice to include my trans status on my Grindr profile. As the messages slowly started to trickle in, I wondered if being openly trans on a gay-only app was a mistake.

'Didn't think I'd find trans attractive before.' I rolled the comment over in my mind, thinking about what he meant by it. I imagine it was intended as a compliment... Like I didn't realize I liked sushi before I tried it, or I didn't realize I liked football before I played. He'd made an assumption and then was surprised by a realization. There's nothing wrong with that, I guess; we're surprised by new things all the time. But it nagged at me. He had made a negative assumption about a whole group of people based on nothing but stereotypes. He was essentially saying, 'I don't find this whole group of people attractive apart from you; you're okay.' That was an unsettling notion. Why should I be an exception? Is it because if I were to walk past you in the street, you would probably assume I am cisgender? In which case, he was saying, 'I find you attractive because you don't look trans.' As if passing as cisgender is good and not passing is bad. Like the holy grail of transness is to look cis. I find this kind of compliment, if you can call it that, uncomfortable. The problem is that trans people aren't cuisines to try, sports to play or objects to handle. We're people. And so the 'compliment' was nothing of the sort. He was making a presumption based on nothing but stereotypes and prejudice and a very narrow view of what men, especially trans men, can look like. And more than that, it was 'trans' that bothered me. Not the term trans, but the use of trans without 'people' being added on the end. It's a real bugbear of mine, and I try to resist gnashing my teeth whenever I hear it. Trans being used as a noun – a thing – an object. It's disrespectful, like we are objects only to be looked at and used. 'A transgender', rather than 'a transgender person'. I know to some it may seem like subtle semantics, but in reality, 'a transgender' positions a person as a thing, whereas 'a transgender person' uses transness as a descriptor of a person with real thoughts and feelings, capable of loving and being loved.

It wasn't just the 'didn't think I'd find trans attractive before' comment (although that would have been enough) that I didn't like; it was the general feel of the app and the conversations that left me feeling like I was doing something I shouldn't be. It felt naughty. And nerve-wracking. And exciting and scary. It wasn't that I'd expected it to be all sunshine and rainbows (pun made and intended), but I just felt like it was a harsher environment than I had imagined, and it was in contrast to what I'd been used to experiencing in a relationship. Like there was no cushioning or kindness. I wondered whether this was just what being gay was – trying to find warmth in cold places. Trying to make ourselves comfortable in the little space we have. All squished together in our tiny boxes, looking but not really seeing the people around us. I wondered if we as gay men realized, or cared, that it could be so soulless, or if that was just something we'd had to become accustomed to, or perhaps we hadn't known anything different.

Budduurrt.

A new Grindr notification. I pressed my screen and swiped right.

Bondage Fun tapped you.

I clicked on his blank profile.

Bondage Fun. 28

Student. Discreet. Kink – mostly bondage. Drop a message and ask.

I swiped away and browsed some of the other profiles on the grid.

Hung Top. 24

Hung top mainly for meets. No pic, no chat. This is non-negotiable. If you start with unsolicited nudes, I will block you. Tall bottoms to the front.

Toby. 43

Drug free. Looking to be entertained.

A. 34

Professor looking 4 dates and wine. Prefer manly. Hygiene is important. Time waters XXX

Throat f*** me. 29

Looking for regular, sloppy deepthroat, no gag. Swallow, FWB, 4.20 Discreet... I'll make u cumm handsfree. Ur human fleshlight can do anal too. No fems.

* * *

It felt like *a lot*. Like a completely new way of communicating and language that I'd heard used before in passing, in jokes or online, but hadn't really seen earnestly and in action. It really isn't the same as Bumble or Tinder or any of the other dating apps. And I suppose, why should it be? Queer people have historically done things their own way, in a way that suits their needs and culture, despite pressure from hetero-normative standards. While I find that admirable, I also felt a bit shocked having never really come across language like this before. The app is really in a league of its own – with its own vocabulary and acronyms and ways of communicating and sharing pictures. I needed to get up to speed, and fast.

The first thing I had to come to terms with was the idea of tribes (as Grindr refers to them). It seems that we as gay men are obsessed with putting ourselves and each other into boxes so we can clearly decipher and filter out the men we're not interested in. Bears, as the name suggests, are an older, hairier, and slightly larger build of gay men. It's a kind of rugged masculine look. Twinks, on the other hand, are young, smooth (and hairless), traditionally slim men with little to no facial hair. Otters are somewhere in the middle. Bears-in-training, if you like. They're hairy, on the slimmer side and tend to be between 25 and 35 – although that's not a hard and fast rule. Discreet – typically men with wives or guys who aren't out yet.

Testosterone, being a strong and dominant hormone, gave me, amongst a deeper voice and receding hairline (thanks), a devilishly hairy bush of a body. I'm a walking carpet, basically. I mean really, it should be illegal. Or I should at least get a token for body waxing or something, more for the benefit of public health than my own. So it feels slightly unfair that I went from girl to otter in matter of two years and completely bypassed my twink years, but I suppose you can't have it all.

Without fail, the third or fourth message after 'Hi. How are you? Good you? Yeah good' is 'What are you looking for?' Now I'll hold my hands up and say I'm guilty of asking this question too. It's a quick way to find out if it's a friends-only, or friends with benefits, or group sex, or open relationship kind of dynamic. I realized fairly early on that I hadn't really given much thought as to what I was looking for and I was at a loss for what to say whenever the question was asked. And that was often. I knew that I wanted to be in a gay space, but that was about it. I hadn't gone one step further to consider what that meant or what I wanted to do in that space. I suppose I thought I'd just scroll from the comfort of my duvet. Maybe I wanted another relationship – although it felt too soon. Or maybe I wanted local friends – connections

– although that felt like it'd be tricky, considering most pro-files were extremely sex-forward. Or maybe I did want sex – although I hadn't had sex with a man before, and the idea of having penetrative sex for the first time felt terrifying.

Thinking about it now, what I was missing was bounda-ries – knowing what I liked and didn't like, what I wanted and didn't want.

I tried to give it some thought. It felt overwhelming to try to figure out what I wanted and didn't want, being so new to the culture and having no experience of gay sex at all up to that point. I didn't know where to start or whether I'd get hurt once I did eventually decide to put myself out there. Still the question remained – and it burned in the back of my skull – would gay men find me and my body attractive?

One late October evening shortly after I had first downloaded Grindr, my date Al and I sat in Comptons bar, Soho. The drinks were flowing fairly steadily and I'd vowed to only have half pints in an intentional effort not to get pissed mid-week and end up dancing with drag queens in the Admiral Duncan opposite *again*. I sat with Al on the comfy seats overlooking Old Compton Street, nursing our drinks and people watching. We watched as the twinks minced by, eagerly watched by the bears hanging out outside the entrance. We saw, too, straight couples looking towards the bustling pub with intrigue and suspicion, seemingly confused as to why just one pub on the street was so full and yet others had seats still yet to be filled. The trans and gay flags adorning the door (the first thing I try to look for when going into a bar for the first time) seemed to pass them by entirely.

Al and I chatted about everything and nothing. Most of our texting had been attempts to get the other to travel to our parts of London – me in West London, Al in south-east and well over an hour away by Tube. Eventually, after a bit of back and forth, we decided to meet halfway in Comptons, a gay pub in central London known as a friendly hang-out spot.

A small group behind us hadn't been so easy on the booze and their conversation grew louder and louder, eventually spilling into ours.

'I'm a platinum gay though. Never even touched one.'

'What?' replied his pal half in disbelief. 'Not even, like, a girlfriend in school or anything?'

'Nope, never. Just couldn't *ever* do i—'

They all laugh.

'Hang on, what's a platinum gay? That's better than a gold-star gay...isn't it?'

'Yeah. Means my ma had me by c-section, so I've literally never even touched one. And I won't be starting now!'

They all laughed smugly again, sipping their elderflower G and Ts.

'Are you alright, Harry?' Al tentatively asked, knowing full well I was not but at a loss for what else to say to address the silence that had fallen between us.

'Yeah. Fine,' I replied, the colour draining from my face. I held up my half-full glass. 'I'm going to get another; do you want one?'

I got to my feet and made my way to the bar, my stomach feeling like I had drunk acid. I stood next to a tall man ordering a couple of pints and waited to be served, pausing a moment to breathe, process and understand what I'd just overheard. I looked back towards at Al, who sat scrolling on his phone, oblivious to the group behind still boastfully and bullishly laughing. Another man walked up to the bar beside me, sandwiching me in the middle, both the men's heads and shoulders now towering above mine. Like that view from the South Bank of London across the Millennium Bridge of St Paul's, which was once the highest point of London, now dwarfed by a skyline of huge offices and tower blocks in the City. I was there, but the size and the confidence of the people in the room made me invisible. The bar member asked who was next, and before I could answer, the man to my left leaned over me and gave his order. I let him, having no real confidence, desire or energy to argue the point.

After getting our drinks, I sipped my double vodka and Coke through a striped straw and watched London grow darker and more alive as the evening fell. The group had long since moved on to a livelier, darker, edgier bar, but I felt their presence remained. I thought about the language they used – platinum gay, gold-star gay – a kind of tiering system or purity award for whoever is the 'most' gay or most thorough, as if it was some kind of competition. After some Googling, I found that gold-star gay meant someone who has never had sex with someone with a vagina. A platinum gay, added later to the dialogue for an extra layer of exclusivity, is a term for gay men who have come into this world via c-section and so hadn't ever been close to a vagina before. When the guys had been talking, they'd almost given these terms a grandiosity, as though it was something to aspire to or a badge of honour. I couldn't help but feel like if I were ranked by them as a gay person who had a vagina, I'd be right at the bottom. Maybe they'd call me aluminium.

I'm not naive to the fact that this was intended as a joke. And on the surface, sure, there have been loads of jokes about gay men not having sex with women and gay women not having sex with men. But the people having this conversation weren't talking about genders, they were talking about bodies. By reducing each other down to only penises and vaginas, we're completely erasing the experiences of women who have penises, men who have vaginas and non-binary people who can have whatever. I find that as a trans person, we're quite quick and adept at thinking, carefully and in real time, about the intention and meaning behind things cis people say. More often than not, we're in a position where if we're misgendered we're told, 'Sorry, I didn't mean to offend,' and we have to weigh up quickly before responding if it really was a genuine mistake (in which case, cool, let's carry on with our day) or whether someone was intentionally misgendering us to make a point. Or when someone makes a 'joke' about transness, we need to be able to make a quick-fire assessment whether they're laughing with us or at us. If they're punching up or punching down. It's a safety defence mechanism. In this particular case, in the case of the platinum and the gold-star and the who-knows-what-other-metallic-tiering-system-I-didn't-hang-around-long-enough-to-hear, it definitely felt like punching down drenched in misogyny, peppered with biphobia, with a pinch of transphobia thrown in for good measure.

By positioning themselves as platinum gays/full gays, they are invariably saying that in order to be a premier gay specimen, you must not have been near a vagina. I'm not sure where in their mind that puts gay men like me, who have not only touched, sucked and fucked vaginas but who also have one themselves.

This idea of what makes a *real* man or woman, and therefore what defines gay relationships and sex, permeates across all kinds of debates and conversations – from university lecture halls to academic literature to fiction to TV shows and, ultimately, to conversations with mates in pubs and when looking for hook-ups on Grindr. And so the question that took up the most space as I was entering this gay new world was: if gay culture is seemingly so phallo-centric, where do I fit, if indeed I fit at all? Will I be welcome and be able to find a place among this community? Will anyone find me attractive? Will I be able to find a home within my own skin?

* * *

6.

Oh you look fun.

Nice pp. Hot.

Ever been a pup for 2 lads?

7.

Afternoon.

U ok?

Looking for 3rd?

8.

Hey

Hey how're you

Yeah I'm good. You're into books?

Yeah, I'm reading Shuggie Bain at the moment.

Oh nice!

9.

Hey what you into?

Hey! I think I'm looking for friends. Maybe fun. I'm kinda new to this.

Oh cool. Don't worry, we have all been new to this once. I'd be interested in both, if you want. Maybe we could do a drink first?

Sure, that sounds good. ☺

When ya free?

10.

Heyy, you good?

You got any pics? ☺

* * *

I'm often asked for cock pics on Grindr. With it being a dating app for gay men, it comes with the territory. It's not intentionally exposing, degrading or even a compliment really. It's just the done thing. Torsos, torsos, torsos. Cock pic, cock pic, cock pic. After receiving a few requests and not really knowing what I should be replying with, given I don't have a cock to take a picture of, I began thinking about what my go-to response should be. Should I ignore the question? Or do a lengthy coming out? Or just say I don't want to send pics? In the end I settled for the simple 'I don't have a dick.' It's short, accurate and, well, I don't have the time for repeated comings out to people who couldn't be bothered to click on my profile in the first place, frankly. Their responses tell me everything I need to know. Without fail, it's one of the following:

1. What do you mean?

2. Okay. What do you want me to call it then?

3. Ignored/blocked.

4. That's cool. I'd like to see more of you.

If it's option 2 or 4, I continue the conversation.

*　*　*

I first came across Arthur on Twitter. He's around my age and a trans man from Peterborough. At the time I scrolled and clicked on his profile, he was standing as the Labour candidate for Paston and Walton ward. He'd sent a Tweet that went viral a couple of months back about the state of the potholes on the roads in his area. He'd filled them with water and placed little rubber ducks in them and taken photos as part of his campaign. I thought it was funny and original, so I followed him. Now another Tweet of Arthur's surfaced on my timeline. *'This has sent me, I'm so glad I downloaded Grindr again.'* Underneath the caption were two photographs, one of a Grindr conversation which read:

cock pic

Don't have a dick

Make one

Next to the screenshot of the Grindr conversation there was an accompanying photo of Arthur holding a plasticine model of a red penis, which he'd made. He'd given it blue balls, with an oddly shaped red bellend. Arthur, with his dry and literal sense of humour, had taken the challenge head on, so to speak. I smiled to myself and liked the Tweet. I think that was the first time I'd seen or heard of another trans man on Grindr. Or another gay trans man at all, in fact. I knew I couldn't be the only one, but it was refreshing to see another trans person acknowledging their sexuality and taking up space on a gay, sex-forward app and being so open about it. Now, I wasn't about to make a plasticine penis and send photos of it to strangers – I could never be that original and who even has multiple colours of plasticine anyway?! – but it was comforting to know I wasn't alone, and it gave me confidence to stay and hope I could find others like me out there.

* * *

When we say the gay community is small, what we really mean to say is it's inevitable that at some point someone you've fucked in the past will become your friend's boyfriend. And strangely enough, that's exactly what happened. And that's how I got to meet Arthur for the first time.

Dan, Arthur's boyfriend, and I lived in the same borough of West London. Dan and I had come across each other on Grindr (of course) and he looked cute. He has spikey hair (in a Ben 10 type way) and made cheeky, confident poses in the mirror. When I zoomed into his picture (because who doesn't?) I could see a rainbow university lanyard (okay, so he's smart), pronoun badges from Lush (it's getting better, not a transphobe and he smells nice) and, more than that, his bedroom was tidy (sold). We started chatting and the conversations felt different to the ones I'd had previously on Grindr. They weren't monotonous or purely sex-charged, they were intelligent and witty, and I found myself chatting to him for days on end. We decided to meet for a wine locally and get to know each other a little better, which resulted in a month-long whirlwind romance.

Such is the way with these things, even though Dan and I got on well and he ticked all the right boxes for me, our chemistry just didn't spark. I knew there would be someone else who would complement his bright, nerdy and charming personality better than I did, so we decided to settle on being friends. And I'm glad we did, because he's now become one of my closest pals, and the fact he's local and can pop round for boardgame night anytime is a bonus.

Dan and I were out with friends at a bar one summer evening when I noticed his phone kept buzzing. That could only mean one of two things: either there was some family crisis or there was a new boy on the scene. The fact he kept giggling to himself and, bless him, trying to be subtle, confirmed with little effort that it was the latter.

'Who is he then?'

'Who?!'

'The boy you're clearly texting!'

Dan smiled. Busted.

'He's called Arthur. He lives in Peterborough, so I'm not sure how we matched, but here, look.' He turned his phone round to show me a picture. 'Isn't he cute?!'

I knew who Arthur was immediately. I'd followed him closely enough on Twitter.

'Oh my God, I follow him on Twitter!' I replied, without a beat.

'So do I! Although he doesn't follow me back, so I've told him off for that.'

The rest of the evening was spent asking Dan about Arthur and what they had planned. I'd never seen Dan so excited, and it was beautiful to witness someone so clearly in the early stages of falling in love.

Dan and Arthur have been pretty much inseparable since, and I don't think I've ever met a couple better suited. It makes me so happy to see how much they care for and look out for one another, always snuggling and holding each other on the sofa when we hang out. It's that kind of infectious, effortless love that just pours from them both.

As it turned out, Arthur and I have a lot in common. We'd

both enjoyed and played football when we were younger, both on girls' teams, but we felt we had to stop when gender dysphoria started to kick in and we started to transition. It's a sad and common thing for trans people to stop exercising when beginning to transition. There are always issues around changing rooms and gendered teams. For me it was more the physical strain of trying to exercise with a chest binder – an extremely tight mesh crop top worn underneath clothing to try to push down boobs to give the appearance of a flatter chest – which made running exceptionally difficult. Admittedly, I probably did wear mine too tightly, but it was a catch-22: wear a tighter binder and look like you 'fit in' or wear a looser binder to breathe better but risk being told you're in the wrong changing room. There wasn't an option really. Binding was as much about avoiding violence as it was about feeling comfortable, or rather, making others feel comfortable around you. And, shamedly, there is still the need to make others feel comfortable. It's a safety concern. Because when people are scared or feel threatened, they attack. My fear of sport as a trans person is not unfounded. A 2019 report by Outsport[1] found 58 per cent of trans people reported feeling unwelcome in sport, with 46 per cent having had a negative experience in sport within the last six months. My only surprise at these figures is that they are not higher.

Arthur had recently moved into Dan's flat in West London and wanted to get to know more people. He'd found an LGBTQ+ football team – The Leftfooters – and had been

---

1   Outsport (2019) 'Sexual Orientation, Gender Identity and Sport.' Accessed on 17/08/2022 at https://leapsports.org/files/1741-Outsport%20 Scotland%20Report.pdf

along to a few of their Sunday friendly games and thought I might enjoy going too.

Admittedly I was nervous about going for the first time. To my own shame, I'd started to internalize and believe unfounded things about gender and my own sporting ability. I feared that I wouldn't be good enough, strong enough, masculine enough. I thought that maybe I didn't possess whatever was needed to be on a male team because I hadn't had testosterone pumping through my veins for my entire life. It's silly really, because I don't apply that same approach to my work. I don't think I'm less good at my job because of my gender; it's irrelevant. So why would the idea apply to sports and things I would enjoy?

Arthur was right. I really enjoyed playing football again. I played terribly, but that wasn't because I was trans, or not masculine enough, or because I have synthetic testosterone injected into me every four weeks – it was because I hadn't played in a decade and I was starting to find my feet – or boots – again. It was affirming playing on a men's team. If anything, it was nice to see that some of the other players were just as bad as I was. But none of that mattered. It was about enjoying the game, not about how well we performed. I noticed that my body moved differently to when I played last time; I was stronger although less agile, and it was strangely comforting to have the ball hit squarely onto my flat chest. It was truly a liberating approach to sport and football, and it offered a new lease of life and possibility for my body. I realized that I'd pushed down any cravings for team sports for the longest time because I assumed that I wouldn't be able to join or that I would not fit in. But I was proven wrong. Here was a team, welcoming to all people willing to enjoy the game regardless of gender and sexuality.

Passing

When we talk about transness we talk of passing. What it means to pass as male or female in society and what it means if we don't. Traditionally, 'passing' as male or female, from a medical perspective at least, has been the goal of transitioning. In the past, 30 or 40 years ago, gender 'specialists' would consider how well a person was likely to pass if they were given medication. If there were likely to pass, then they'd be offered hormones and encouraged to live their life and to tell *nobody* about their past. Just quietly drop their whole experience and existence and live as an entirely new person from that point on, as if that is easy. If the trans person seeking help was deemed by medical professionals as not likely to pass enough, medical support and intervention would not be given. Trans people in dire need of help, support, love and understanding were left desperate and alone because they were seen as people who would not fit comfortably in society. They would bend the idea of what it means to be a man or a woman too much, and that, these professionals felt, was a threat.

When I started Googling trans stuff on the internet, there were many blogs and articles about how a person can pass better. For example, articles on websites by other trans people suggested wearing a white T-shirt underneath an unbuttoned shirt to give the illusion of a boxier, square shape to hide any curves. The article encouraged us to hide under layers and layers of fabric. There were voice-training activities, too, so we could train ourselves to lower our voices, make-up tutorials that taught us how to use mascara to give a five o'clock shadow, shoe insoles to give more height, plastic packers shaped like penises to insert into underwear to give the appearance of a bulge. Everything was about trying to appear as cisgender as possible. It was less about feeling comfortable within ourselves and more about not making others around us uncomfortable. In short, it was about hiding ourselves and our transness for the benefit of cisgender society.

Nowadays, whilst passing still plays a part in transition and is what *some* trans people strive for, it's not a universal goal. I'm pleased to see more trans people being openly non-conforming and loving their bodies, including their hips and breasts, and celebrating themselves for their transness, not for how well their bodies pass as cisgender. Passing, thankfully, is no longer a marker of success. In part, this is thanks to the work of the author Juno Roche, who writes with candid honesty about her feeling of having a hybrid body – a trans body that exists outside of binary male and female. When her work was first published, it really changed the game for how trans people think about our transness and what it means to us, rather than what it means for cisgender people. Hers is a thorough, honest and nuanced understanding of gender rather than simply the male-to-female or female-to-male phenomenon that was often depicted by British press in the early 2000s. It's also thanks to authors, playwrights and po-ets like Travis Alabanza, whose intelligent understanding of gender and race has led to many ground-breaking moments for cis and trans people, myself included. Travis's work is direct. Their play *Burgerz* was one of the first plays that really expanded my (and many others') view of gender and what it means to be a trans person – and in Travis's case, a trans person of colour. *Burgerz* looks at the violence of gender in its various forms. Not just physical attacks – like how an unknown assailant threw a burger at them in broad daylight during a transphobic attack in London and passers-by did *nothing* – but also the violence of the confines of gender. Of how there are two boxes – male and female – and if we do not fit, we are forced to bend, mould and squish ourselves in until we break. Travis's work is clever and confronting, peppered with charm and wit. But it also asks the questions many trans people have not dared ask – like what could gender be if we did it on our own terms, rather than within the claustrophobic constraints that have been inflicted upon us since birth?

More recently, I've seen a strong reclamation of beau-tiful trans bodies in the work of Ezra Michel. He's an Ins-tagrammer, music-maker, model and hairdresser. After his top-surgery scars faded, he decided to get them tattooed. A thin, black line is inked over his top-surgery scars on both sides, curving up slightly at each end. When asked why, he said that he missed the visibility of his scars. He said they were part of him. They were his story. His history. He didn't want them to fade. He said that it was a kind of power, an opportunity to remember the strength and resilience of his own mind and body, and how we can bend and make our-selves into something stronger. For him, his scars are part of his joy rather than pain and they are not something to simply be massaged away. They are something to be shown and celebrated. I couldn't agree more. Since then, Ezra has modelled in waist-slendering corsets, showing off an hourglass shape cis men could only dream of achieving. He's fashioning typically 'female' clothes in a transmasculine body and distorting notions of binary gender. I relate to this so much. Because as a young person I was viewed as a girl and a woman, there were clothes that I didn't want to wear and couldn't feel comfortable in, like dresses or heels or tight tops. Now I am comfortable in my gender and I know I am seen by the world as male, I don't feel confronted by traditionally female clothing. I can happily play with gendered clothing and it doesn't threaten my sense of self. I can wear a skirt and heels and still be seen as male without it feeling confusing. Playing with gendered clothing and being referred to by other gay men as 'she' is a huge part of gay culture. And so it's affirming rather than confronting to play with these gender presentations.

In the last year or so Ezra has launched his own US-based clothing brand called PUSSY BOY of the Revolution. When I saw it I thought, 'Yesss!!' Finally, we're being brave enough to stand up and say that transness is not only about wanting a certain body part or wanting to get rid of another. Being transmasculine doesn't just have to be about wanting a dick. Some people do, some people don't. Our masculinity and experience are so much more than our genitalia. And we can celebrate the bodies we have rather than the bodies we do not.

The word pussy, for many trans men, can make us feel uncomfortable. It's gendered and can be quite harsh – especially if we remember that word being battered haphazardly around the playground by teenage boys trying to assert their new-found power and hypermasculinity. I know of a few people who squirm when they hear the word and can't say it out loud. That's understandable. For some people, their bodies give them an immense feeling of discomfort. But for me, I feel there is power in reclaiming these words for the bodies we have and saying, *'Yes, I am a man and I have a pussy. And you know what? I like that. I enjoy my body. It makes me feel great and I will not allow you to take that away from me.'* What Ezra is doing *is* a revolution because it is so far away from what cis people think of transness and even what some people within our own trans community view transness to be. There are so many conversations and battles we have with ourselves about who is trans and who is trans enough. Can you be trans if you want hormones but don't want a dick? Or if you don't want hormones but you do want top surgery? Or if you are trans but don't want to pursue any medical diagnosis or intervention at all? And here is Ezra, breaking so far away from the relentless policing of bodies and saying, 'I am going to do what is right for me. I will embody, embrace and enjoy this amazing trans body I have been gifted.'

I am comfortable and happy to say that I am a pussyboy – a part of the revolution. I don't want to have bottom surgery for reasons that are my own. I exist in the world happily as male, and the genitalia I have don't make the faintest difference. I'm claiming it. It's ours. We can celebrate ourselves for the people we *are*, not the people we *might* become. We are saying we do not need to scar ourselves or need to change if we don't want to. There is so much strength in that.

* * *

I don't aim to pass as cisgender. It's no longer a goal of mine. I don't wake up any more and think, what can I wear that would make me pass in the street so people will call me 'sir' or mothers can say to their little ones, 'Mind that man coming through'? Yes, that used to make me happy in the early days when I was still figuring all this stuff out. But I no longer let other people's view of me dictate my own sense of self or self-worth. I just wake up, put on what I like and wear what I feel comfortable in. Whether that's a packer, or a shirt with a T-shirt under it, or, fuck it, short shorts, heels and a tank top.

I know I 'pass' as a cis man. I know this because whenever I come out to new people they look shocked and say, 'You'd never be able to tell!' as if that's a compliment. But the difference is that I no longer try. It's not a goal or aim. I don't seek to be cis because I am not. I'd be denying the endless possibilities of my body. And the very act of *not* denying myself feels revolutionary and important because for so long trans people have been told to push, stretch, scar ourselves until we are fixed. I no longer want to be seen as fixed because I am not broken.

I'm very conscious that unless I wear a T-shirt that says 'I'm trans' or wrap a humungous Trans Pride flag around my waist, I pass. To society, I'm cis until proven otherwise. I'm cis as default. If we went back some years ago, back to when medical professionals were telling people this is how we must be, this would have been great. Job done. Fixed. But we've not yet had the conversation about how invisible passing can make someone feel. Passing is an assumption about your life so far and how you have experienced and do experience the world that isn't the truth. And transness is all about truth. Personally, I think we should replace the phrase 'pass as' with 'mistaken for' to get to the real root of the problem. As a trans man who has been on hormones for over seven years, I am often mistaken for being cisgender. I acknowledge that this comes with a huge degree of external safety and comfort, but it has also screwed with my sense of self over time. Being seen as a man, as if this is the person I have always been seen as, means so much of my personal experience and history is missed and looked over. My experience as a trans man is completely inconceivable. My experience of being trans is hidden in plain sight. Sometimes I want to scream, 'I'm here, I'm here, I'm here. I exist. I exist!'

A little while ago I was at a gig on the South Bank. I was supporting a friend at a show; she's in a group of four women who sing about growing older and being a bit naughty and silly. It's funny and empowering for them. They have a collective age of around 280 and sing retrospectively about the menopause and tackle many of the taboos and misogyny they have faced in their humorous, and sometimes raucous, music. It's a fun show. They have a huge number of supporters, especially women who can see themselves in their humour. After the show we had celebratory drinks. One of the lead singers, who I'd not met before, said, 'Oh, it's hot in here! It's probably the menopause, not that you guys have to worry about that.' The male friends around me laughed. I laughed, too, but what I wanted to say was, 'I do worry about that! I don't have the body you think I have! I'm here, I'm here!' It's lonely and difficult to be invisible. And the ironic thing is that so much of their art and music is about exactly that – feeling invisible as older women. I wanted to say, 'I understand! I'm invisible too!' But that's the point, isn't it? To be invisible is to be on your own. After that moment had passed, I wished we could have recognized each other and understood that we are more the same than we are different. I wish we could have held space for one another. I hope that next time we can.

*   *   *

I once overheard a conversation in Evelyn's Tea Rooms Café, an artisan coffee shop in Manchester's Northern Quarter. It's the type of place non-millennials would take to Twitter to rant about. House plants, avocado on toast and some of the most delicious vegan dishes around. I was sitting on a wooden seat looking out of the window – always the best spot – waiting for my friend to arrive whilst reading *A Little Life* by Hanya Yanagihara, which meant I was feeling *very* emotional. The two guys behind me were laughing and flirting outrageously. On any other day I would have found it heartening, almost cute, but today I didn't.

I overheard one say to the other, 'Yeah, I was fat back then.'

'Were you?' the other asked with earnest surprise.

'Yeah. You can see there.' He picked up his phone to show a past photo of himself. 'See? Fat. Love handles. Proper birthing hips.'

They both laughed.

I did not laugh. Not because I wasn't at their table and it would have been rude to appear to have been listening in, but because my heart sank so far into my gut that when I took a breath again it felt sharp. 'Birthing hips' was being used to describe a state of being that is undesirable. I'd go even further to say it was emasculating. A hippy curviness rather than the 'ideal' wide-shouldered, small-waisted, typically male 'V' figure. I have birthing hips. Literally an hourglass figure that can give birth. No amount of cardio, running or Zumba can change that – I know because I've tried. It's just my frame.

I felt upset that my body was seen as laughable and I would never be able to reach the 'V' shape, no matter how hard I tried. I closed my eyes and yearned for smaller hips. Pined for my hip bones to be shaved and scraped away.

* * *

I don't feel alone in being self-conscious and critical about my body. Many trans people are. Many cis gay men are too. Fuck it, most people are, aren't they? There's a huge pressure on us all to be 'perfect'. For me, the pressure is to pass, but not too much. Queer but in the *right* way. To be gay, but not *gay-gay*. Not a vodka-cranberry gay, or a football-and-ale gay or a dancing-queen gay. Matthew Todd discusses this best in his book *Straight Jacket*. He says that gay men are at real risk of being overly critical of themselves and their bodies, which, if they are not careful, can develop into behaviours that are difficult to manage, poor mental health and low self-esteem. He says 'heterosexual attraction is a state of being attracted to "the other", whilst homo attraction is a state of attraction to "the same"... In homosexual attraction, there is, on some level, an act of direct comparison.'[1] It's this comparison, he notes, that can be even more tricky to navigate. For me, I'm not 'the other' in the way that Matthew refers to, but neither am I 'the same'. I can compare myself to cisgender gay men, but the painful truth is that this is an unattainable, impossible goal. I do not have a cisgender male body. So any comparison (which I involuntarily make all the time) leaves me feeling that my body is not good enough. No amount of protein shakes, mornings in the gym, face masks, waxing

---

1   Todd, M. (2016) *Straight Jacket*. London: Bantam Press. p.163.

strips, surgery or moisturizers will give me the body I have desperately craved for most of my life. I know this because I have tried most of them.

It's an odd dichotomy. Even though I'm viewed as cisgender by much of society and my transness is overlooked, I do not come close to having the body of a cis person. I am expected to act like I had a boyhood. I am given quizzical looks when I queue for the cubical and I can see people asking themselves, 'Why isn't he using the urinal?' It's awkward. We are told that we do not know what it is like to have periods or hormonal imbalances such as the menopause. We are told that we cannot be given emergency contraception because 'Boys do not get pregnant.' Our reality as trans men is entirely missed.

Did I ask for this? Is this what I wanted when I signed the forms and took testosterone for the first time? Maybe. Was I doing this for myself or for other people? I don't know. I wanted male characteristics, sure. I wanted to be masculine when I looked in the mirror. I wanted to see myself on the outside as the person I am on the inside. But I never asked for my reality and history to be erased entirely. I don't want to pretend like I didn't go to a girls' school, or that I didn't play netball, or that I don't have a pussy. My girlhood (as I saw it at the time) made me the man I am now. In fact, more than that, my girlhood made me a *better* man.

When a Stranger Called Me a Faggot

'd planned to meet my mum for dinner in August of 2021. It was her birthday and she'd come down to London especially to celebrate. To mark the occasion and to get out of the grubby jeans and T-shirts I'd been wearing most of the week, I decided to dress up and try a new outfit. Something a bit different, something special, a bit more out there. It's good to shake up the wardrobe sometimes, isn't it? I pulled my blue-denim high-waisted jeans up, rolling them several times at the bottom to show off my sparkling white Converse. Then I put each hand into the arms of my shirt – a black-and-white polka dot flimsy blouse that fitted me just right over my shoulders. I tucked my blouse in a little at the front, leaving the rest to flow down, and opened the shirt buttons on the front to display my gold necklace. My hexagonal gold earring matched perfectly and hung proudly in my left (gay) ear.

I crossed the zebra crossing not far from my house on my way to meet Mum. It's a busy road, and the cars drive well over the 20-miles-an-hour speed limit and always seem surprised and pissed off when someone wants to cross. On this particular occasion, I was standing alone at the crossing, waiting for traffic to stop. A car and a white van stopped to let me pass and I thanked them with a reach of my hand as I started walking to the other side. Before the van began to move, the driver pulled down the passenger side window. My stomach churned. I felt on edge. *He's just pulling down his window to get some air*, I tried to reassure myself, although it wasn't very convincing. *Walk with your head high, Harry. You have nothing to be ashamed of.* Even as I rolled those words around my head, I could feel his eyes burning into my skull as I crossed. I felt self-conscious and sped up, my feet moving double-time.

'Bend that hand a bit more and you might get some, faggot!' he yelled in a gruff, harsh voice.

There we go. That was it. The thing I simultaneously anticipated and feared.

At first I was taken aback. I'm often nervous about getting shouted at in the street, and I tense up and prepare the best I can in the little time I'm given. My heart starts to race, my palms sweat and my body fills with adrenaline – I'm ready to fight or flight, but nine out of ten times nothing happens. You prepare and psych yourself up only for it to dissipate moments later. But this time it did happen, and although my body had prepared itself, my mind hadn't, so it took me by surprise.

I've had homophobic abuse and slurs thrown at me before, but not as a gay boy. Before and in the early days of my transition, I mostly encountered lesbian-specific homophobia and criticism for looking butch. Whenever I encountered homophobia like that, like the time Lucy and I were holding hands at Twickenham station and a man shouted, 'Come on girls, give us a kiss!', I'd be really upset. One, because it felt sexually violent, and also because I felt protective over Lucy. It felt as though men had the entitlement and ownership over women's bodies to say and do whatever they liked. In some ways the misgendering felt even worse. I was presenting in a masculine way not because I was butch but because I was a man. The fact that this was missed could sometimes hurt more than the homophobia itself. It was a reminder that the outside world did not see me in the same way I did.

This time, however, was different. Being called a 'faggot' out of the window of a van didn't have sexual undertones in the same way. It felt harsher, rife with disgust. My experience of lesbian-homophobia was that it always carried a 'come on love, you're not a lesbian, you just haven't had the right dick yet' kind of dismissive, condescending and entitled undertone. Now, my experience of gay male homophobia is that the people delivering it really want to hurt you in a vicious attack and feel no accountability at all. Both instances are horrible and leave a bitter taste for weeks, sometimes months, after.

'Bend that hand a bit more and you might get some, faggot.' I replayed it in my mind. I tried to understand what it meant beyond the homophobic language. Was he suggesting that I looked gay (hand bent) but not gay *enough* to be fucked? Or maybe he was saying that I looked too gay and he was being sarcastic? Was it a warning? That if I appeared more gay, I'd be at risk of sexual assault or something?

I thought I'd feel upset at someone calling me a faggot and being mildly sexually aggressive. But as I continued to walk and meet Mum – because what option do you have other than to continue – I found myself feeling mildly amused. I'd wanted to be a faggot my whole life. Seen as an openly confident gay man. I'd worked hard – coming out, navigating arduous gender services, medically transitioning, going through a breakup and doing so much soul searching to understand my gender and sexuality – to be called a faggot. And now, clear as day, here was confirmation that finally, I was seen at first glance by the outside world as the gay boy I have always been. It was, in its own strange way, the affirmation I wanted.

Of course, if I had a choice, I wouldn't be shouted at in the street. Nobody would. A concerning report by the Home Office shows that homophobic and transphobic hate crimes have risen year on year since 2019.[1] I see more often now than I did before tweets and conversations about friends being called faggots on the street and pictures of violent attacks against gay and trans people. It's a real worry to see this increasing trend, and although I got off lightly that day I crossed the road, there are so many people that don't.

During lockdown, I remember reading a tiny extract in the news that a gay man was murdered in Tower Hamlets cemetery, a well-known gay cruising spot. At the time, that was the closest park to where I was living. I knew things were starting to get really bad when, in 2019, images emerged all over the news and social media of two women who were brutally attacked on a night bus as they were travelling to Camden Town. A group of men had been throwing coins and making sexual gestures before they began beating them with

---

1   Chao-Fong, L. (2021) 'Recorded Homophobic Hate Crimes Soared in Pandemic, Figures Show.' *Guardian*, 3 December, 2021. Accessed on 17/08/2022 at www.theguardian.com/world/2021/dec/03/recorded-homophobic-hate-crimes-soared-in-pandemic-figures-show

fists. 'There was blood everywhere,' one of the victims said.[2] It's sobering that in London, thought of by many as one of the most accepting places for queer people, there is so much more to do to tackle LGBTQ+ hate crimes. In July 2022, trans man Noah Ruiz was arrested for using a women's bathroom at a campground, despite being told by the camp mangers that this was the best toilet for him to use as he hadn't physically transitioned yet. After a confrontation in the bathroom, Noah was beaten, 'choked until his face turned purple' and a guy 'was telling me he'd kill me, calling me a fag'.[3] Noah was arrested for disorderly conduct. His aggressors didn't face any charges.

To be LGBTQ+ in the UK, and around the world, is to be in a relentless hurdle race. More hate and obstacles are thrown if an individual has an intersectional identity. Say if a person is trans, gay, and subject to racism and misogyny. Trans people of colour in particular face hate crime and violence more than any other section of our community and, worse still, there are few outlets reporting on these abhorrent crimes and few groups supporting these individuals.

To me, transphobic violence doesn't always necessarily mean being shouted at in the street. Violence takes many forms. Yes, physical – sometimes – but what of the violence of this government, who seek to put intentional and unnecessary barriers into legal recognition as male or female? Or

---

2   Hunte, B. (2019) 'London Bus Attack: Arrests After Gay Gouple Who Refused to Kiss Beaten.' *BBC News*, 7 June, 2019. Accessed on 17/08/2022 at www.bbc.co.uk/news/uk-england-london-48555889

3   Factora, J. (2022) 'This Trans Man Was Just Trying to Pee. He Was Assaulted and Arrested.' *Them*. Accessed on 17/08/2022 at www.them.us/story/trans-man-noah-ruiz-was-just-trying-to-pee-he-was-assaulted-and-arrested

of intentionally removing trans people from a conversion therapy ban, throwing the doors wide open to psychological torture and abuse for people who are not ill and do not need fixing? And what of medical violence? Choosing to continue having huge wait times (currently up to five years) for specialist care, making trans people jump through high, unfounded hoops that fit a strict narrative of what it is to be trans – gatekeeping life-saving hormones and surgeries. And what of police violence? Our Prides did not start as a celebration; they started in direct resistance to the police raiding our bars and arresting us for the crime of love. And what of employment violence? Companies outing employees and dismissing them unfoundedly – like in the case of Julia Grant, a caterer for a London NHS hospital, who was outed to her employers, and had her career threatened for *daring* to transition.[4] And what of the violence of erasure? Stonewall recently won a campaign calling for lesbian, bi and trans people to have equal access to IVF treatment, but the published document made no reference to trans people at all – refusing to recognize trans people as human beings and people who are capable of wanting children in the future. And what of the violence of being trans? When we were born, a decision was made for us without our consent. We are forced to live childhoods alien to us and become girl to woman, boy to man. We are told not to ask, not to question, that this is just a phase, to push ourselves down, to damage, bend and break ourselves until we fit. To be trans is to face violence while

4   BBC (1980) 'A Change of Sex, Episode 1: George – The Big Decision.' Accessed via BBC iPlayer on 20/09/2022 at www.bbc.co.uk/iplayer/ episode/p04frg16/a-change-of-sex-1-george-the-big-decision

others 'yaaas queen' and 'sashay away' using the language of our ancestors while ignoring our struggle.

For some, trans lives are something to be debated over Sunday dinner. A 'But should trans women be allowed in women's toilets though?' throw-away question over a roast chicken and cranberry sauce. But real lives are at stake. To be trans is to face violence but be a warrior. We navigate systems that are not designed for us. This doesn't mean that we are wrong. It means the systems in place are. And we will continue to fight and change them.

A Trans Man Walks Into a Gay Bar

I grew up in rural Lancashire, in the north-west of England, and as a teenager, I occasionally took the hour-long X43 bus from Burnley Road into Manchester, making sure to stay on until the very last stop – Chorlton Street. It was completely unnecessary, having already trundled past the shops, restaurants and cinemas, all the places where I planned to meet my friends. But Chorlton Street was the entrance, like a dark mouth – alluring and terrifying in equal measure – into the Gay Village. The bus would hiss as it lowered to allow passengers off, and the driver would mumble that this was the last stop before switching off the dim yellow interior lights. The Manchester rain would batter against the pavement below and day-tripping nans and mums with colourful polka-dot prams would depart into the city. I'd be sure to take my time getting off the bus, not to keep away from the rain, but to stay as close to the Gay Village as possible. Sometimes, when the weather was better, I'd circle the perimeter of the Village on foot, daring to be near but without the confidence to step inside. It was the fear of the unknown mixed with the idea of being met with people whose identities confronted my own. Being in close proximity to a queer space meant seeing lesbians, gay men, and trans and queer people of all varieties, which I adored in one sense, but in another, this revealed identity conflicts I had yet to address or fully understand. I was met with people whose dress, interests, behaviour and quirks were entirely different to any I'd experienced in the small town I grew up in, yet I felt a kinship to and understanding of my own identity and with how I wanted to be perceived by the world. I found it confusing. I wanted to be like them but didn't really know how.

Occasionally I would spot queer people walking hand-in-hand towards the Village, heads high. I longed to be like them: older and knowing. The rainbow flags were visible, vibrant and inviting despite the pounding rain, but my shame and shyness held me from inching any closer. Pleasures just out of grasp. I wanted to proudly walk into the Village and down Canal Street like them, but my lack of know-how and confidence (plus, I had no knowledge of the bars, and I didn't have anyone to go with even if I did) meant I kept my distance.

On the outskirts of Manchester's Gay Village there are small signs on lamp-posts that read, 'Welcome to Manchester's Gay Village', which feel more like a warning than a welcome. As if the signs were saying, 'Come here, but at your own risk' or 'You may find people or scenes here upsetting' or 'These people are different, beware' or 'Don't look this way, it soils our perfect, serene heterosexual landscape'. I found these warning signs, the spatial segregation, othering. Like the rest of the city is the same, but queers are different. It was both frightening and enticing in equal measure. I found myself growing hungrier and more intrigued to experience what was on the other side.

I'm pretty sure a lesbian couple must have once clocked me glancing longingly when perched at the bus stop. They threw me a knowing, friendly look. I felt almost see-through, like I could hide from the world but not from them. Somehow they knew I was queer; they recognized my trepidation and tentativeness. I wondered how many other people had made this pilgrimage, circling around the Village but too afraid and full of shame to enter onto the queer cobbles. I may not have known what my identity looked like at the time, but I did know for certain that I was queer in some way. And that in the future, after I'd overcome my initial apprehension, Manchester's Gay Village would become my home and the people within it my extended family.

It was rare for me to go into Manchester, as I was fully embroiled in countryside life and the bus at £10 return was expensive. Every trip into Manchester almost felt like a trip to New York, an urban exotica, so far removed from my experience in the country that it hardly felt an hour away at all. Going into the centre of town felt transgressive, alternative, hectic and volatile. No passing tractors or waiting for fleecy sheep to cross the road. It was honking cars and too-busy-to-stop pedestrians, assumedly on their way to All Bar One to gossip about how Casey was such a cow to Connor last night, or something.

After my admittedly tentative pilgrimages around the perimeter of Manchester's Gay Village, in the summer of 2013, having just turned 17, I decided to go to Manchester Pride for the first time. I was lucky, I suppose, that Manchester was close enough to journey to by bus, even though culturally it felt a lifetime away. I didn't wear anything particularly Pride-related or 'out there' – certainly no glittery shorts, rainbow T-shirt or kink harnesses like I would now – out of fear

I'd get ridiculed or punched on the way in. Remember, I'd had fireworks thrown at me, and the memories of being cornered in the changing rooms at school because my classmates had feared me to be a lesbian were still buried in my mind. After that, I didn't take any chances wearing an overtly queer uniform or colours. Instead, I wore blue jeans and a zipped grey hoodie – drooling, bland colours rather than brilliant rainbow ones. Clothing with neutral territory, not male, not female, and toned down as much as I could.

I watched the gorgeous, glistening, glimmering and glinting parade from the sidelines of Market Street. I saw exultant and cheerful faces, hearts beaming with pride and love. I saw for the first time that gay really could mean happy. I sometimes hear gay people describe gay clubs and Pride as 'safe spaces', to which I think, 'A safe space is at home watching *Schitt's Creek* for the fourteenth time with a packet of milk chocolate Hobnobs!' Now I can feel 'safe' in some gay spaces, but only because I've become accustomed to them. On first glance though, they can be intimidating.

Manchester Pride showed me first hand what the inner cogs of Manchester's Gay Village might look like and that there are so many ways to be queer. Whether that be an elderly gay man at the front of the parade riding his scooter with a placard reading 'the oldest gay in the village', or a gay family with adopted children, or a gay couple in matching tank tops and high-waisted jeans, or an 85-year-old trans woman with her girlfriend; there were so many ways to be.

Stickers from all groups and charities walking in the Pride parade took shelter on my T-shirt that day. I gathered flags, stickers, whistles, anything I could get my hands on from the LGBT Foundation, *Coronation Street*, NHS Pride and so many more. The irony was that the bland clothing I had intentionally picked to blend into a crowd had in fact made me stand out. I was the only person not wearing vibrant and fun-filled clothing. The only grey cloud in an otherwise clear blue sky. And so the stickers, the whistles, the temporary tattoos were a welcome addition, a kind of welcome pack patchwork quilt.

Not wanting my queer enlightenment to end too soon, I bought a last-minute daytime ticket into the Gay Village after the parade. Pride flags adorned the place, and the once-bland gravel NCP car park had been transformed into a huge stage featuring artists and performers. I wasn't sure if it was my anxiety, the gorgeous men in glittery hot pants or the bass of the music rippling through my body that caused my heart to beat furiously. Either way, I felt electric. I could see gay girls and guys kissing and holding each other without having to glance around or be nervous if it would cause offence. And swarms of friends basked in each other's company. It was nothing other than blissful, a celebration of love in all its forms, and for a variety of ages too. It was a space to simply be. Far away from a heteronormative world that tells queer people that we are sick, disordered, morally evil individuals who seek to promote and recruit others to a 'gay agenda'. As far as I could see, the only agenda was to love. I saw nothing that was sick, was morally evil or promoted a so-called lifestyle 'choice'. It was absolutely and implacably happy. I saw people enjoying and owning their bodies, choices and destinies, whose only ambition in life was to achieve love. I felt sad that queer spaces are the only places where some LGBTQ+ people feel they can express themselves, and outside of these places feel we need to tone down or self-censor. For me, I felt I could be myself amongst others who truly 'get it'. I realized that gay clubs, pubs, cafés and bookshops are not just places to pull pints or meet each other, they are refuges that serve nectar to our sense of self and our cultural identity.

*   *   *

Going into a gay bar now as a single gay man is completely different to what I had experienced at Manchester Pride when I presented as female. It was almost as if they are entirely separate spaces. Now, being in my early twenties and living away from my parents, I am actually looking to pull, for one, but more than that – I have noticed men look at me differently. Well, actually, not just differently. Men actually *look* at me. I am not completely brushed aside (sometimes literally) and ignored. At Manchester Pride, before my physical transition, men would largely disregard me. I guess they assumed I was a lesbian. Now I feel like they have begun to take notice. They don't push past me and push me out of the way at the bar. They make conversation while queuing to wash our hands in the toilets. One guy offered me poppers on the dancefloor. Now men let me pass and offer to buy me drinks. Now I was a man, I was visible to other gay men. I acknowledge the misogyny in this and wonder if they ever notice how much lesbians were getting pushed around and made to feel as though gay spaces are only for men. I wonder if they'd ever really taken the time to consider what it might be like for anyone else who isn't cis or male. I felt guilty when I realized I also felt affirmed by gay men now recognizing me as one of them. I liked the feeling of being *seen*. I promised myself that I would not be the same, and I use my experience of being pushed, of being ignored, of being othered, to allow space for others.

If I imagine the last queer bar standing, it might look like the Royal Vauxhall Tavern (RVT). It's been there an age – since 1863 – and in 2015 was given Grade II listed status, the first of its kind for LGBTQ+ heritage spaces. It was a destination point for post-war entertainment, specializing mostly in cabaret and drag, and it sits south of the river Thames, alone, on the corner next to the railway arches. It looks as though any buildings that may have been to either side of it have long been demolished, but the RVT remains defiant and strong. The Vauxhall Pleasure Gardens, to the right of the RVT as you look at it, has long been a place associated with queer culture. In their book *Vauxhall Gardens: A History*, David Coke and Alan Borg suggest that the first appearance of a man we know to be gay in Vauxhall was at the exclusive Ridotto al Fresco ball, which launched the refurbished Pleasure Gardens in 1732. For a visual, think *Bridgerton*. John Cooper, a well-known homosexual better known as Princess Seraphina, visited the ball in a calico gown, mob-cap and smock and paraded around the gardens. Looking through an alternative queer lens, some historians suggest John was perhaps the first transgender or drag appearance in Vauxhall, rather than the first homosexual man. Words to describe trans experiences didn't exist then, so people weren't able to describe themselves as such – and even if they could, they would put themselves in serious danger – but that doesn't necessarily mean that these identities weren't experienced. All too often, men who wear feminine clothing are quickly assumed to be gay men in history books. It's only now with better understandings of trans and queer experiences and language to help explain how we feel that we are able to look back into history and pose questions to our queer ancestry. Clearly we are not able to ask John Cooper how they would describe themselves with today's language, and I wouldn't want to put words into their mouth, but I think it's fair to assess that there was a queer identity there – whether that be gay, trans or drag. Reaching into the past to understand and question our queer elders is important for me to find my place and put together a sort of patchwork of queer ancestry. Understanding our past helps us better understand our present and our future.

I chose to go to the RVT for my first gay boy night out because I was attracted to its rich heritage. I felt a sense of belonging and place and it comforted me somehow. You can almost feel the secrets seeping from the brickwork and red structural pillars that support the building. These pillars were once on the bar top, and drag artists would swirl their bodies around them, using them as props and supports for their performances. I had first heard of the RVT in a documentary on Channel 4 about cruising. I can't remember the name of the documentary now, but I remember the archive footage they showed from the late sixties and seventies. I watched it late at night under the safety of my duvet as a teenager, and I see this now as a touchstone moment for my sexual awakening. It was like nothing I'd ever seen or heard of before. Cabaret artists pranced and paraded up and down the bar top in ebullient dresses singing at the top of their lungs. Men would watch in awe and cheer before moving into the shadows to suck each other off outside, cum drooling onto the pavement. There would be coded signals and Polari spoken and police raids on this underground secret drag operation... Even if this is a fetishized idea of what this space was like, I still find the story and essence of it exhilarating. It was 'wrong'. It was filthy. It was exactly the kind of night out I could only aspire to. It was, and still is, a fearless space. Where people can be together without oppression or intimidation, and experience their and other people's bodies, and music, and lighting in various stages of intoxication and sexuality. At the time I didn't know why I watched it or what had encouraged me to find and click on the documentary in the first place. It wasn't necessarily the men that lured me in, it was more the place, and I felt a pull and feeling of belonging to a venue that I'd never been to before. It was curious. I didn't know how or why, but I knew I wanted to be there.

It was my first night out in the RVT as a gay boy and I successfully pulled the hottest boy in there. Win. It was the RVT's famous and long-established Dukie night. I must admit, it is rare for me to just clock eyes with an attractive man in a club and get off with him there and then. I don't want to paint myself as someone who is confident enough to do this regularly; I think I just got lucky. There was a drag artist who was performing a set about Twiggy. They had mixed sixties pop music to audio bites of Twiggy's critics, who were condemning women for wearing short PVC mini-skirts. It was a great set, raucous and so, so much fun. I looked up at the stage, eyes glistening, in my absolute element. A boy, maybe three or four metres to my left, was doing the same thing. We had been making eyes at each other all night between getting drinks at the bar. His was a Camden Hells, mine, a double gin and tonic. It's always a double, darling. He was tall, dark and handsome. Not in a heterosexual James Bond kind of way – he was weedy looking and wore rounded tortoise shell glasses and hoop earrings with a sort of mullet at the back. He was a pretty boy. Exactly my type.

His brown eyes flared as the act made their exit, and he turned to look at me, eyes catching and holding on to mine.

I felt my body and face blush. I held my gaze back at him. I swallowed and gripped onto the red pillar next to me like a life raft. He moved closer, and as the DJ set began, we danced together, our hips moving and chests pumping, smooth as synth. He shouted in my ear in his luxurious Irish accent and asked for my name. 'Harry,' I yelled. 'Yours?' I asked, my voice getting louder. His name got lost over the music and truthfully, I probably wouldn't have remembered it anyway. I was far too distracted by the fragments of glitter on his arched cheek bones. It was something beginning with J, I think. I nodded in that polite way you do when you can't hear anything but pretend you know what a person is saying.

We danced. The lights encouraged us and so did the alcohol. Our lips pressed together, heads turning to get a closer touch, the stubble of our beards nuzzling each other. I could feel his glasses pressing into my cheeks. My eyes closed and the world span as fast as the disco ball above. The unrelenting bass beat pumped through my bones as I raised my hand to his neck, fingers running through his thick, dark hair, sticky with gel. His tongue slid across mine, snaking around my mouth, his hands moving around my body, finally resting on my waist. I could feel his hips against mine and his hardening cock through his blue-checked trousers. I kissed him more, noticing how my body longed for his.

We got a cab to mine at around three. It was that time of the night when suddenly the dancefloor empties and you know there's nothing to gain from staying. The bartenders look exhausted and the queue for the toilets takes an age. If you haven't found what you're searching for already – a boy, a dance, escapism, drugs or whatever else – it's not happening now.

I'd told him I was trans on the dance floor, just before I'd asked whether he wanted to come back to mine. 'I'm a trans man,' I said, surprised at how confident and matter-of-fact I sounded. There was a time when that would have been the hardest thing in the world to say. There were a couple of beats between us where our shoulders shrugged with the music. 'That's cool,' he said. 'I know already. I follow you on Twitter.' Fucking hell. I know they say the gay community is small, but Christ. How much did he know about me? Did he know what books I'd read recently or the gig I went to the week before? I made a mental note reminding myself not to share too much online. Still, I relaxed a little. I had been dreading the inevitable, awkward dance floor coming out. When's the right time? Before you kiss? You don't want to assume they want to get with you in the first place. Post make-out? It feels too late if we've already made moves. In the cab? That feels too dangerous – they're literally on the way to your house and there's no getting out on the Wembley bypass. Just before sex? Well, I didn't want to get myself in too much of a vulnerable position when telling someone something potentially surprising to them. You never know how they might react.

It's not fair that we constantly have to out ourselves like this. Cis people don't go round the dance floor telling each other what their genitals look like, when they got them or what they like to do with them. They'd probably get kicked out if they did, and rightly so. I suppose cisgender people don't have to. It's that cis-until-proven-otherwise thing again, isn't it? Cisgender is the expectation. Even queer and gay people who are educated and welcoming and knowledgeable about trans people still assume cis until proven otherwise. We live in a cis-until-outed world. Unless they follow you on Twitter and you constantly make trans-related quips and share topless photos of yourself, that is.

It was a mixture of excitement and nervousness as we got a cab back to West London. I didn't even think about how much it was inevitably going to cost, which is rare for me. London living on a low salary is not the one. I'm a fierce saver. As the noise from the Tavern grew distant, I found myself trying to think of something to say. Something to fill the 40-minute journey back. I think he was musing the same thing because neither of us said much. Instead we held hands, hidden away from the driver in the dark, taking what opportunity we had to continue the intimacy from the dance floor into a contrasting, quiet space. We continued to hold hands, gently stroking each other's fingers, the confirmation we both needed that this – whatever it was – was still happening.

I hadn't had sex with a guy before. Well, not properly anyway. I'm not sure an 'is it in yet? Fuck I've gone soft now' experience in a tent, aged 17, quite counts. I wasn't completely naive to what a penis looked and felt like. I had seen plenty in real life and in porn; they just hadn't, you know, gone in. My stomach filled with anxiety and I worried. I worried if my body would work, or if my pussy would just seize up as it had done the last time. I worried if it would hurt. I worried that if I told him that he'd be annoyed at me for being practically a penis-virgin. People in their early twenties are usually much better rehearsed at this. I worried about his size – if he was really big...or if he was really small. Or if the condoms I had were in date. Or if he'd agree to use one anyway. Or if he couldn't cum. Or if I would enjoy it. Or if he'd ever been with someone with a pussy before or if all this was completely new to him too. I worried if I'd remembered to make my bed. And if there was anything in for breakfast tomorrow. And fuck, what was his name again?!

I turned to face him. He'd fallen asleep, his hand still in mine and his head gently rocking on the head rest. Street lights flashed through the window as the cab twisted through silent residential streets. The light speed bumps woke him just as we arrived at my flat, the taxi making an abrupt stop. We got out of the car, thanked and paid the driver, who shot me a knowing, cheeky look as I fumbled in my pocket. We made our way to the flat and I turned the key in my front door.

* * *

We woke at 7 a.m. The sun was just creeping around my window blind and the morning light spilled onto my bookshelf. My head pounded. How is it that whenever I'm hungover I wake up earlier than I do on a work day? Typical. It was mostly quiet, except for birdsong that was interrupted by the slamming of car doors on the street and kids on their way to football practice. I rolled over and felt him beside me. He was sleeping peacefully on his back, one arm bent above his head to cover his eyes and shield them from the light. I watched as his chest moved gently up and down. As I gazed, I noticed something I hadn't the night before. Small, sharp hairs were beginning to poke through the skin of his chest. He'd clearly shaved or waxed it recently – three or four days ago, judging from the growth. I wondered whether he liked to be smooth, or if he'd spent time in the shower shearing himself in anticipation of a hook-up. I imagined him in the shower, lathering shaving foam over himself and delicately scraping the razor against his skin, letting the hair fall to the bottom of the shower and clogging the plug. I glanced down at my own unkempt chest foliage. I wondered whether I should have shaved my chest too.

He stirred, moaning slightly as he moved onto his side, his face now turned towards the wall. He pressed his naked cheeks into me. I pulled my arms around him carefully and he welcomed my warmth. I kissed his neck and put my head onto the pillow next to his, considering when the best time to wake him would be. How long does the morning after a hook-up usually last? As I held him, our bodies intertwined, I could feel parts of myself that would usually go unnoticed. There was an emptiness between my legs, and I wondered what it would have been like to have awoken hard. What it would be like to have his cheeks brush against the length of me.

It was comforting to wake up next to someone handsome. It felt like I'd achieved something. As if my pulling of an attractive man enhanced my own sense of worth, desirability and masculinity in some way. It gave me a sense of affirmation and new-found confidence.

After twenty minutes or so of cuddling, I began to grow restless. The morning was calling me, so I went into the kitchen and brought back peppermint teas in matching floral mugs into bed for us both. I woke him by running my fingers through his hair and kissing the side of his neck.

'A peppermint tea?' I asked. He nodded, beginning to sit up. 'Thanks, that's really sweet.' His voice was deep – husky-ish – and that made him all the sexier.

I could have lain in bed with him all day but I knew I couldn't – I'd already promised a friend we'd meet for coffee – so I reluctantly and lazily made my way to the shower. By the time I'd washed, brushed my teeth and dried off, he was already up and pulling on last night's clothes. 'Thanks for such a good night. I had fun.'

'Me too. Thanks for looking after me.'

'No problem. Shall we do this again?' he asked.

'Sure,' I said a little too quickly, admittedly liking the feeling of someone wanting me. 'That'd be nice.'

'Great, I'll message you. Thanks for the tea.'

After he left, it was as if my bedroom had become a new space. Now it'd been christened by a handsome, erudite boy and was not just harbouring long-exhausted memories of a breakup. It felt lighter, and I lay on top of my bedsheets thinking of him and the night we'd shared. How I had been surprised by the softness of his lips and the gentleness of his hands as he searched my body. How effortlessly he'd opened the button of my trousers, allowing his hands to cup my pussy, not showing any hesitancy or faltering. How he had asked if I was okay before he opened his lips and sucked on me, treating every mouthful as if it was his last. How, when he pulled the condom onto himself, covering himself in lube and throwing the empty packet aside, it was as if he was doing it to care for me. As protection. His shape thrust slowly into me, opening me up, and I moaned – not because I was closed or sore, but as a signal for him to move deeper, which he did, kissing me, his tongue searching to find mine.

*   *   *

My first sexual experience as a gay man had been a success. It didn't matter that I never saw him again. It didn't even matter that we'd hardly spoken afterwards. What mattered to me was that I'd broken out of the fear of having sex with gay men and that my first experience had been so relaxed and joyful. That, despite the chip-fat-haze drunkenness, I felt wanted and cared for. Sex had been about each other's pleasure rather than what body parts I did or didn't have and what that might or might not mean for his own sense of identity. In the end, it wasn't about transness or cisness. It was only about enjoying each other and the pleasure we could give. When it really got down to it, it was just us in the moment, focused only on making each other feel desired. Wanted. Two men needing each other. The pieces finally fitted together.

We all place expectations on other people. In part, this is based on what we put out into the world. For example, if a person wears a band T-shirt – Primal Scream, say – then yes, it's likely that person likes the band. But it also connotes something more about their character, like they might have grown up listening to the band in the nineties, they prefer beer to gin and tonics and they probably listen to Radio 6 Music. Now, these are huge generalizations, and of course they won't be true of everyone, but our expectations and assumptions about people are a shorthand to try to understand their character and make quick-fire judgements to establish if we might get on or if we might be a threat to one another. It's primitive. Then, when we get to know that person better, we may cast away any preconceptions and be happy to be proven wrong or surprised – maybe they don't drink alcohol at all or deep down they might really love Radio 2. We're often happy to understand that this is *our* misconception and judgement and to be proven wrong. However, the same doesn't seem to apply to sex and gender. If I present as male, which I do, it's expected that I have a penis. These are judgements that other people have made about me, rather than claims I have made or something I have lied about. Yet if I come out as being trans and I hadn't told someone straight away, this is often seen as something I have been disingenuous about. That I've been intentionally secretive to try to fool someone. As if I owe it to everyone to tell them my genitalia when we first meet. It's absurd. For that reason, it can be incredibly nerve-wracking to tell someone you're trans because it is often believed that we have in some way tricked them, disguised ourselves and misled them. Sometimes this leads to rejection and someone saying they're no longer interested or, at worst, can put us in real danger. We see the playing out of angry 'reveals' in the press all the time and it's been going on for decades. In 1981 the *News of the World* outed Caroline Cossey in a headline that read, 'James Bond Girl Was a Boy: Topless Tula hides sex change secret.'[1] Subheadings including words such as 'fake' and 'shocked' questioned Caroline's authenticity. When helping to clear out my grandmother's house following her death, I found a *Daily Mail* article from 1998 that read, 'The Boy Soprano Who Was a Pregnant Housewife…"They were being fooled. For he was really a she."'[2] And more recently, on 8 May 2022, the *Times* ran the article 'Trans Status of Recruits "Must Be Disclosed to Employers": Women's groups worried about self-identification reforms raise safeguarding concerns over job checks.'[3] All of these articles perpetuate a notion that trans people are a façade, hiding themselves, and therefore a threat and danger to others. Could it not simply be that we, trans people, are just trying to get on and live our lives?

---

1   Fae, J. (2018) 'The Press.' In Christine Burns (ed.) *Trans Britain: Our Journey from the Shadows.* London: Unbound. p.190.

2   Scott, R. (1998) 'The Boy Soprano Who Was a Pregnant Housewife.' *Daily Mail*, 3 April, 1998.

3   Macaskill, M. (2022) 'Trans Status of Recruits "Must Be Disclosed to Employers".' *Times*, 8 May, 2022. Accessed on 20/08/2022 at www.thetimes.co.uk/article/trans-status-of-recruits-must-be-disclosed-to-employers-dp9lfzqh6

When looking for a partner, I always come out to them at the earliest opportunity. This is not because I feel I should, or because I think it is the *right* thing to do. If anything, I believe I shouldn't have to. Why should I? I'm not tricking anyone or being disingenuous; I'm just being myself. I shouldn't have to wear a T-shirt that reads 'man with pussy'. But I do come out because it helps limit any hurt or rejection I might get further down the line. It's a protection mechanism, really. I hope that in the future we get to a point where it isn't necessary to come out over and over again for our own protection and for the comfort of cisgender people. I hope that we reach a moment where we don't assume that everyone who dresses in X way has these genitals or someone who wears Y has those ones. It's up to us all – trans and cisgender folk – to catch ourselves when we're making these assumptions and judgements and to treat people as just that – people.

But Who Will Love You?

During the process of writing this book, I've really had to examine why I was so worried and fearful of meeting gay men and being intimate with them. I think it's reductive to say it was purely because of my breakup with Lucy. Or that because I grew up as a girl, I've witnessed and experienced the ways in which the patriarchy does harm. Or because I imagined being the only trans person in a room full of gay men would feel lonely. Or because all this gay stuff was totally new to me. Or because dating, sex and allowing yourself to be vulnerable, regardless of gender and sexuality, is objectively terrifying. In reality, it was a mixture of all these things.

I've learned (after a considerable amount of therapy) that my fear of having sex with men and of dating comes from a fear of rejection. I don't think this is unique to me. None of us want to be rejected, do we? Being human is all about finding 'our people' and 'our community'. Or our 'pod', as my mum calls it (my mum *loves* orcas). I heard the chant 'show me what comm-uni-ty looks like? *This* is what comm-uni-ty looks like!' on a trans rights protest march recently and it filled me with pride. It feels so empowering and encouraging to be part of something. Whether it's a religious group, football team, the LGBTQ+ community, a book club...whatever. It's human to want to belong. I was hesitant about putting myself 'out there' and meeting men because I worried that we'd meet and then realize I wasn't funny enough, or attractive enough, or knowledgeable enough, or experienced enough. Too fat, too thin, too masc, too femme, too political, not political enough, too serious, too young, too old, too short, too Northern, not Northern enough, too shy, too confident. I'm sure many people feel like this about whatever insecurities they hold. But above all insecurities, my main fear was not being 'man enough'. And therefore, I worried I'd be rejected for something that feels as natural to me as my eye colour. I wasn't worried about my character, per se. I'm pretty self-assured in my masculinity in that sense, but it was my physicality. A gay boy with a pussy. Our hypersexual gay world rewards and encourages the 'perfect' male form – tall bodies, thick shoulders, thin waists, hairy but not too hairy, long, thick cocks...you get the idea. The beau ideal. Any deviation from this leads to a risk of rejection. If you look at gay websites or magazines, or just log onto Twitter or Instagram really, you'll find (and it'll probably be what you're after) endless images of perfect bodies in sexy pants. It doesn't show the variety, expanse or possibilities of what gay bodies do and can look like. And over time, what that does for our community is that it tells us that we are not good looking enough, thin enough, buff enough, gay enough, man enough, if we don't look like this. It seeps into our consciousness and it really affects our sense of self and cuts away at our self-esteem. It's a compare and despair cycle.

Rejection is familiar to me. Trans people often face rejection – from family, friends, colleagues, healthcare and political structures – so much so that rejection from others almost feels certain. We come to anticipate it happening again and again...and again. As I walk into the doctor's waiting room or my local pharmacy, I feel my muscles tense and shoulders rise as I prepare to fight for and justify my existence. My body prepares to battle in case I need to fight (again) for a prescription for the hormones I've been on for the last seven years. Resistance is in every fibre of my muscles. My body prepares itself without me even realizing in case the GP or pharmacist says that they're 'not comfortable' prescribing or dispensing this medication, or, 'We need to get you in for blood tests, which might take four weeks, before we can consider issuing another prescription.' All the while, I face the risk of my medication just being...stopped. Which, if it happens, means I am in danger of de-transitioning. It's a terrifying prospect to be faced with. All these things have been said to me by medical professionals on numerous occasions. I'd go so far as to say that they're said to me on a regular basis. So every interaction feels more like a wrestle for accessible and humane healthcare. It can be difficult, not to mention exhausting, to constantly put yourself out there, fearing and anticipating the worst. With every exchange we have to prepare for picking ourselves back off the ground afterwards. It makes us hardy, but God it's exhausting.

* * *

The thought of going on dates and meeting up for sex was a real challenge for me. It not only meant the usual hurdles, the ones we all go through – the worry about meeting someone new, whether we will get on, what I will wear, if they will like me – but additional, higher hurdles with myself too. Things I had to wrestle with before meeting up even started. Like do my hips look too wide and feminine in this shirt? How will this person react when they're met with my pussy and the reality of what I look like? Will they see me as their equal, as another gay man, or an imposter?

Being in a relationship or getting married is seen in cis and heteronormative society as a hallmark of success. How many times have we heard from parents or grandparents, 'Have you found yourself a nice girlfriend yet?' or 'When you have kids of your own...' or 'Have you thought about engagement yet?' and 'You should think about finding someone nice and settling down'? I've wondered why this is. I think it might have something to do with acceptance. Acceptance by yourself, by your family, by neighbours...by society. If you're in a relationship, you're good. Someone has chosen to be with you so that must mean you're alright. If you're single for a prolonged period of time, then that must mean something's wrong; there must be a reason why another person doesn't want to be with you. This is such a heavy pressure to put on someone. Sometimes people don't want to be in a relationship, or they're not ready, or they want to travel, or maybe they're not romantically or sexually attracted to anyone. We're all so fixated – myself included – on finding someone so others can accept us and, ultimately, so we can accept ourselves. When I was younger and upset, I used to cry, hold myself and repeat, 'It's okay, because Fran fancies you, so does James... That must mean you're okay. Other people like you, so you're okay.'

I don't think the pressure parents or family (or we) put on us to find someone comes from a bad place. I think they just want us to be happy. Find someone to go to your cousin's wedding with, or to the cinema, or to cuddle into at night. That's not a bad thing to want for your children – companionship. But for queer people of all flavours, it can feel burdensome. All I wanted (and if I'm being honest, what I still want) is to be liked and to feel like I am part of the group. The hard part about coming out to myself as gay and trans was that I felt it was a threat to being liked. Who would like, or love, me if I was different?

I came out to my parents via letter. I like to think it's because I'm an old-school romantic and the type of person who buys parchment and nice pens, only to never use them in fear of ruining their lovely newness, but actually it was because I was scared. I knew that if I sat down to have that conversation, I wouldn't be able to say all the things I needed to. I'd shy away, terrified, and therefore intentionally miss all the difficult bits out. The only way I could explain, in full, was through writing it down. That meant that once the letter was handed over there was no going back. Major respect to anyone who said those words, 'Mum, Dad, I have something to tell you.' You have more strength and bravery than I do. I didn't have the courage to do that. So a letter it was.

It was a warm day in late August 2014, just after my 18th birthday. The trees were rustling and casting crisp, beautiful shadows on the tarmacked road. My hayfever was playing up and I sniffled all the way back home from the village fete. The realization that there was no 'right time' came from seemingly nowhere. I hadn't really been thinking about my transness or coming out. I'd just been focusing on getting ready for university. But maybe that was it... Maybe subconsciously I wanted to begin a new life in London, with new classmates and friends, as someone who felt authentically me. It was a perfect, sunny day, a rare occurrence in Lancashire, my parents and I hadn't argued in a while, the family were all in good health. It struck me that if today wasn't the 'right time', then when would be?

The letter itself was surprisingly easy to write. I'd known I was trans for a few years by then and had wondered how I would come out – if indeed I ever would. I hadn't rehearsed anything or thought about what I wanted to say. The words just flowed from me onto the Pukka Pad in scribbly, spider-like handwriting, full of spelling and grammatical errors. Frankly, if my mum read the letter and decided only to pick me up on my spelling of 'definitely' (always with an i, Harry!), then that'd be a success.

It was three back-to-back pages in total. Explaining that I'd known for a while. That I was hurting and I'd known I was a boy for as long as I could remember. That it was only now that I had the courage to tell them and found the words. I was ready to start pursuing medical transition and find happiness within myself. I intentionally ended the letter with no name, only three kisses. That was my way of being considerate – deliberate love but choosing not to use my previous name, nor the new one I'd chosen for myself, either. I wrote that I was ready to be happy and I hoped they would support me.

I tore off the pages, folded them neatly and placed them into an envelope, because I'm classy like that, and went downstairs. My mum lay on a sun lounger with our dog, Sandy, at her feet. My dad was cursing the lawn mower. My mum smiled when she saw me.

'Can I get you a cold drink, darling? I'm having an iced tea.'

'No, I'm okay... I just came to give you this.'

'What is it?'

'Just read it.'

I turned and walked back into the kitchen and up the stairs to my bedroom. I didn't want to stand there. I didn't – couldn't – watch the reaction. I knew they needed space and so did I. I sat on the edge of my bed looking out of the window onto the driveway and I waited, heart racing, processing what I'd just done and how my life would now change.

The day felt different now – sunny, exactly as it was before, but a heaviness filled me. I was shaking. In truth, I hadn't really considered how they'd react. I hadn't thought that far. I knew they wouldn't throw me onto the streets or anything, and my parents had always supported me so far, but there was no real telling with something like this. This was new territory for everyone.

I heard movement downstairs. My mum must have finished reading it. Fuck, fuck, fuck. Silence.

And then the stairs creaked.

Someone was coming upstairs.

When the door opened, I was surprised to see it was my dad. He was crying. The second time in my life I'd ever seen him in tears. He hugged me. If we said anything, I don't remember it. All I remember was feeling him close to me and a deep sense of relief.

Then, the door went. My brother wasn't home, so it could only be someone going out. The familiar sound of the car ignition started. My dad and I were both surprised as we watched my mum drive away.

I think it was a few days until my mum and I talked. Or maybe it was later that day. I can't really remember. It was all such a blur of anxiety and creeping around the house trying not to draw attention to myself. I felt that if I disappeared, it might be easier.

When we did eventually speak, whenever it was, it was with warmth. It wasn't until that point that she told me that she'd gone to visit her life-long friend to try to deal with the shock and heartbreak. My mum, nervously, sat beside me on my bed and asked many questions. I sensed she was just trying to understand. She confessed to how she had actually gone to our GP about it once. A few years back. She had explained to our family doctor how I'd been struggling with my gender and had wanted to wear boys' clothes and asked if that meant anything. Apparently, the doctor had said that it's a common thing for girls to go through, that it could be a phase and to just wait and see. Then, when I'd begun to date boys, my mum had just assumed that it had gone away. Now she was upset because she could see that it hadn't.

We both cried – her with tears of fear and I with tears of relief. She asked me about what it meant for my sexuality – which was a valid question because I didn't even know the answer to that myself. I said I didn't know. She asked how someone could know they're a boy or a girl, and what that means. I replied, 'Well, how do you know you're a woman?' She answered, 'Well, I don't. Or I do. I just am. I haven't really thought about it.'

I let that rest. 'Well, I've had to think about it a lot.'

We sat in silence.

My mum's worry, as it turned out, was about if transitioning was the right thing, if I really knew and if I would come to regret it. Would this mean I would change drastically from the person I was and would anyone want to be with me if I was trans. 'But who will love you?' This will make it harder for you, who will want to be with you if you're like this...that type of thing. I don't think this was meant in a cruel way, no matter how hard questions like this are to hear. My mum knew that the world is a hostile place for a trans person, or anyone 'different', and she didn't want my life to be harder than it needed to be. That's a nice thing for a parent to want. An easy, love-filled life. She wanted my life to be one of fulfilment and happiness. That's all any parent wants really, isn't it?

I thought about that question: but who will love you?

It struck me as an odd question to ask because I had never seen myself as someone who was unlovable. I see myself as someone filled with joy who has plenty of love to give, and someone who is open to receiving love in return. I always sensed that my core reason for being was to love and be loved and show care and compassion to everyone and everything around me. The idea that a person may not want to be with me because I was trans, and not because of who I am as a person, hadn't really crossed my mind until then. Slowly, I started to unpack the question.

I thought the 'but' at the beginning of the question was interesting and important. It suggests that if I thought a bit harder about the impact of my being trans, and of someone not being able to love me because of it, then I might change my mind. 'But' is a connector, a conjunction, used here, seemingly, as a plea to stop being trans because (as the question connotes) nobody will love me if I am. It plays into the very human fear of ending up alone. The 'who' is rhetorical and incredulous – my mum was already assuming, because of her own fear, that nobody would. It was her fear projected onto me. A fear that I for a long time had internalized and have had to work really hard to overturn.

As kids we're taught that whatever our parents say and do

is right. As adults, we learn that they are just as right, wrong and flawed as the rest of us. I'm very pleased to say that on this occasion, I did prove my mum wrong. I am lovable and people can and do fancy me. I'm not saying this to boost my sense of ego or to show off, but because so much of the fear in people coming out as trans is that other people won't accept and embrace them. I'm here to say that they can and do. Transness is not a limitation to love, sex, dating or otherwise. The answer to the question 'But who will love you?' is: plenty of people! Yes, there may be people in this world who are transphobic or have a narrow view, but there are equally plenty of people who aren't. There are many people who are open, and kind, and willing to learn. And the people who are transphobic? You wouldn't want to date them anyway.

I've often wondered why 'But who will love you?' was one of the first questions asked of me. In truth, I think it was because up until that point I had experienced life being treated and educated as a girl. We live in a patriarchal and misogynistic society in which one of the most important things a woman must concern themselves with is finding a partner. We're taught this from childhood. We're given dolls who cry and need milk as toys when we're little. We're encouraged to play 'house' and dream of a domestic life. We're given little plastic kitchen sets with matching utensils to play with and encouraged to think about cooking future meals for our future husbands. We're taught to apply make-up at school when the boys would learn from local entrepreneurs. We're told, 'You'll understand when you have children of your own one day.' And if we reply with, 'I'm not sure I want kids of my own', we're met with the response, 'You'll change your mind when you're older.' Our narrative, our place in the world is set before we've even thought for ourselves what we would like or we're able to tell people that we feel otherwise. I think the reason *Don't Tell the Bride* is such a successful television show is because society knows that most women think and dream of this day for most of their lives in a way cis men aren't encouraged to. So handing that power over to a man to plan their wife's 'big day' is almost always a disaster for her. She's been planning her wedding for her lifetime; he's been planning it for two weeks. My coming out then, was a disruption of this traditional narrative of 'girl meets boy, gets married, has kids, lives happily ever after, let's ride off into the sunset' fever dream. If my success as a person, as a woman, was dependent upon finding a partner and marriage, then my transness (to them) meant I had failed.

That's essentially what I think that question was rooted in, knowingly or not. A fear and projection that my transness meant I was unlovable. Except I don't see and never have seen my transness as a failure or any kind of setback. Nor does it mean that I won't or cannot experience love, heartbreak, sex or marriage. I see my transness as a gift. An opportunity to step away from the tired and unreasonable expectations forced upon us by societal pressure to fit in. If I do ever have children or get married, it will be because I feel it is right for me, not because it is my place, or because it is what is expected of me. Being queer, gay, trans is freeing in that respect. Our relationships and connections can be formed by what we *want* them to look like. That is a beautiful, delicate thing and something to cherish.

* * *

Despite the initial shock I faced coming out to my parents, we are now the closest we have ever been. It's taken time. I'm calmer and happier because I'm not concealing and fearful of my own nature, and my mum and dad can see that transness is something to celebrate, not something to be scared of. It's taken years of therapy and listening to each other to get to the point where we are now. These days my mum comes with me to Pride and wants to stay out later than I do. She offers to stand my ground to the Practice Manager at the doctors' when they're refusing to dispense my hormone prescription. She was with me when I walked to my top surgery, and my parents were the first people I saw when I woke up. They support me in everything I do.

When I talked to Mum about how she felt on the day I came out she said, 'It was the expectation thing really. You imagine so much for your child as a parent – what you'll be like when you grow up, what you'll wear on your wedding day...children, jobs and things. It was a kind of grief letting all that go. To imagine something different. It took me a long time to realize that I wasn't losing anything or anyone at all. I was gaining someone happier. And really, I had to realize that that's all I care about. All the other stuff – the jobs, a wedding, the relationships you might have...none of that matters. Not really. But I had to learn that. And that was hard. That's why I'm now on that Parents of Transgender Children Facebook page. I don't post much now, but there are parents on there who are scared and worried like I was. And now I can reassure them that it's okay.'

Now when I go to trans rights rallies or Trans Pride Brighton, I see so many parents who are supportive of their trans children. It makes me so joyful and hopeful for the future, as well as feeling an inkling of sadness that it wasn't like that for me and still isn't like that for many. Just last week at Sparkle in Manchester, I saw a parent with a six-year-old who was wearing a sticker with they/them pronouns. It was hard to believe. I didn't even know what the word trans was or that there was any possibility beyond male or female until I was 15. It's amazing that some parents are open to allowing their children to explore their gender and taking them to events like this. It genuinely makes me optimistic. But I also realize that there are many parents and trans kids who will struggle. Especially in rural towns like the one I grew up in. My parents' first real exposure to trans and gay people was through me. There was a lot of learning to do. There were so many questions to be asked and societal assumptions to be confronted. I can completely understand that some trans people don't want to go through this process with their parents. It's hard enough to navigate coming out, healthcare, changing names, employment and physical transition without trying to educate family at the same time. But for me, I wanted to be close to my parents again. And for that I knew I had to be patient and honest, no matter how hard the questions were. But that doesn't mean I did away with all personal boundaries. If anything, the strength I had to turn around and say, 'No, I can be loved' and 'Yes, I'm sure about this – I will do this with or without your support' has carried me through. And there is the power in being trans.

As I look to the future generation of trans people, I hope they don't have to be so hardy and tough round the edges. They will always have strength and resilience, yes, but I hope we can create a world where they don't have to wear so much armour. I hope the strength in their bodies is from playing sport and living long, happy lives, not from fighting battles and justifying our very existence. That's what I see when I look at trans kids being lifted onto the shoulders of their parents during Pride marches. I see the possibility of a brighter and better world. One in which trans people can simply be.

The Ponds

Walking past on the grassy bank of Hampstead Heath, you might miss the men's pond. You need to look out for the heads bobbing, torsos floating and feet teetering on the platform edge, ready to dive in. It doesn't matter what time of year you go, you'll catch swimmers bathing all year round – even when ice skims the surface. The Highgate Men's Pond is renowned. It's a natural bathing bond in the middle of one of London's ancient heaths and is, for me, the most serene place in the city. There are three ponds – the men's, the women's and a mixed pond. The men's pond is the largest, the women's is the most concealed and the mixed is the most open. The men's pond has been popular among gay men for as long as it's been open – which is ages. The 17th or 18th century, I think. I'm sure people used to go swimming naked there and sunbathe on the bank. Of course, Hampstead Heath is already known for cruising – George Michael made certain of that – but there is something more relaxed about the pond. There might be, on the odd occasion, a bit of cruisy behaviour and looking, but mostly it's about men enjoying and experiencing the outdoors together. As so many male-only spaces revolve around pubs, alcohol and sex, I think it's good that men have a healthy, relaxed place to hang out.

The pond is quite large and well managed by the life-guards who keep a careful eye on things. In the outside changing area there is an old sign, which must have been there for decades, that reads:

COSTUMES
MUST
BE WORN AT
ALL TIMES

Usually an older man sits undeath it, man-spreading with hairy bollocks on display.

The pond was the first male-only space I went to and, understandably, I was nervous. Swimming, and indeed any place which involves changing rooms and bodies, is something I find tricky. Being a trans man with scars sewn across my chest, curvy hips and a lack of bulge means I can feel uncertain and worried in male-only spaces. I worry about my place there being questioned and how my body compares to others. It's not that I'm not proud of my trans body – I am. The effort put in to sculpt and mend my body into something I can call home is the greatest act of self-love I have achieved. But still, it's daunting. I see so many cis bodies, the shapes I desperately crave but can never have, and it can feel confronting. But I didn't want to spend my time being preoccupied and self-conscious. I just wanted to enjoy a swim. I tried to remember that 'men-only' space doesn't mean 'penis-only space' and that there are so many variations of cis bodies too. And that like me, others were there for a swim, not to judge. They probably had just as many hang-ups about their bodies as I did. I acknowledged my fear, mentally packaged it up and chose to put it to one side. Being a queer person makes you good at that.

I went to the ponds with a few friends I'd made on Twitter who are also gay. It was a warm, sunny day, late summer in 2019, and we thought it'd be a relaxing thing to do, far away from the other option of facing the crowds in Covent Garden trying to cram onto what little roof-top garden space there is.

In the changing room, we put our bags on the bench and hung our towels up. The boys started to get undressed, pulling their shoes, socks, shorts and T-shirts off. I couldn't help but notice that their bodies really were lovely. Not muscly, but toned, their legs thick with hair, strong chests. As they took their briefs off, I deliberately looked down and concentrated on getting myself changed.

We headed in the direction of the concrete platform, our bare feet feeling the gravel beneath. It felt almost as if we were in the wild. I turned to the little blue shed on my right where the lifeguards sat and watched on. The notice read:

Water temperature: 20 degrees.

Nice.

As I walked onto the platform, I took a breath of fresh air and let it fill my lungs. I'd read online, years ago, that a cis man's body tends to have a triangular shape; their shoulders are usually the widest, narrowing to their hips. In contrast, the hips of cis women's bodies tend to be the widest. As I walked to the platform, my feet familiarizing themselves with the gravel beneath, I couldn't help but notice my own body and the way it moved. My hips felt as if they stuck out, far from the rest of me, and I ached to shave them away, to sand them a little. I'd had top surgery, but there were still parts of my body that I found difficult to live in at times. As I reached the platform, I inhaled, just as I'd rehearsed at home, my chest and shoulders growing a few inches, allowing my hips to sink slightly into shadow. I held the air in my chest and stepped towards the water.

Lowering myself into the ponds from the platform was slippery. Algae had formed around the bottom of the steps and I slipped a little, forcing my body to fall into the water quicker than expected. My ankles met the cold first, followed by my waist, chest and shoulders. The temperature change of the water forced me to exhale the air I'd stored in my lungs quickly, as if the water was convincing my body to relax.

In the water I felt like everyone else. Just a head bobbing, my hair gently patting the water's surface. As I trod, I became hyperaware of how thin the water felt. Not full of chlorine or chemicals – purer than that. I spread my fingers apart, allowing the water to brush between my fingertips.

I can understand why many trans people avoid swimming. I did, too, before I was on testosterone and had top surgery. I was a real water baby when growing up, always wanting to be in the pool. I could be in there for hours – playing, splashing, swimming. But then when I started to transition, the changing rooms became tricky and difficult. I didn't know what to wear – swimming costumes were for women, but men's shorts wouldn't cover my breasts. A mixture of both just didn't feel right for me. It was easier just to avoid the situation entirely. So I quit the school swimming team and didn't return to the poolside for five years or so. Now, in the pond on Hampstead Heath, I could feel the sun's heat on my shoulders and I cherished how good it felt. To not have any swimming costume imprisoning my shoulders or sweaty fabric cupping my breasts. I noticed, too, how my chest hair moved to the rhythm of the water. I moved my chest from side to side, watching how the hair danced and followed the small waves I created. I smiled.

I kicked and swam over to the boys who were together, their hands clinging onto a buoy. It was nice to fully stretch my arms and crawl towards them, my body having a distant memory of stroke technique. As I reached them, we splashed each other and turned to watch a guy about to dive into the pond. He looked like he knew what he was doing – arms outstretched and together, knees bent slightly. Then he did a bit of a jump and ended up belly-flopping in. We looked at each other, taken aback by the sound. The two pigeons who were floating on the surface flew off, disturbed by the inter-ruption too. We giggled. This was good. This was freedom. This was the happiness I'd worked so hard for.

Although getting out of where you're swimming is in-evitable, it always comes as a surprise. I don't like leaving knowing the joy I feel in the water. But as my skin wrinkled, my legs tired and the gossip grew thin, we knew we needed to leave. I hoisted myself back onto the steps, pulling myself up and quick-stepping my way back into the changing room, reaching for my towel at the earliest opportunity.

As I towel myself off, I am aware of my body again, and the bodies of those around me. Men are sitting, both with and without clothes, taking in the sun. One man's reading the paper. Another is whistling in the shower. Why do men *always* whistle? Irritating sounds aside, they all seem at peace. I breathe slowly, trying to allow myself the same.

The boys towelled themselves off and we shared shampoo

and body wash. I noticed my scars were a little redder than before. I made a mental note to moisturize them when I got home. The boys were looking fresh and their long, wet hair dripped onto their sexy, topless torsos. Eventually, we sat together, towels curled around our waists, and allowed the sun to dry our bodies. It felt nice to have a towel around my waist because for so many years, I'd put my towel underneath my armpits to conceal my boobs. I'm reminded of these subtle but significant differences I've made in my life since surgery. And how it's still the little things – the towel around my waist, my shoulders unrestrained by a swimming costume, my chest hair being pulled in the direction of the water – that bring me so much joy. I looked up to the sun and let it hug my face for a moment. I left the pond through the gates, feeling taller and fuller than I did when I entered.

As queer people we often talk of resistance: a force pushing in the opposite direction. For gay and bi people, this resistance is against heteronormative standards. For trans people, it's against cis-normative society and expectations. And for me, it's both. Resistance can take many forms – a protest, a tweet, lobbying government for change, a petition, Pride parades. But resistance is in joy as well as struggle. My resistance is allowing myself to take up space in male-only spaces, like the men's pond. I allow myself to swim and feel closer to myself, even though my body is not what cis society expects it to be. My happiness, the joy I can find in my body, is in itself a force against people who tell us we cannot have these things. That trans people should not be allowed in these spaces because for some reason our existence is seen as a threat that must be challenged. I like swimming. My body belongs in the pool and pond as much as anyone else's. I've realized that queer resistance can be found in the everyday. For me, swimming *is* my resistance.

Since coming out as gay, trans and queer, I've looked at swimming in a new way. As a teenager I'd done that thing we all do on holiday: look in awe at half-naked bodies in the pool or on sunbeds and start to realize what we do and don't find attractive about other people. For me it was flat chests and torsos and boys playing and splashing in the water with other boys. It was as much about the boys and their bodies as it was about the presence of two (or more) semi-naked boys together. It was the first time I'd really been exposed to boys and bodies in this way. When speaking to gay friends, many have said that the swimming pool was formative and important to them beginning to understand their sexuality too. They could openly enjoy the presence of other semi-naked men in a space where it was acceptable for men to be half-naked and playful together. It's an allowable place to look and be looked at.

Swimming by its nature occurs in a littoral space, a place on the edge of water, something that exists outside of normative, acceptable standards in society. This is important, especially for gay men, because homosexuality was illegal under the Sexual Offences Act until 1967. Even then, any intimacy between two men must be in private and for consenting men over the age of 21. Swimming and the shore then, were the only places where gay men could be with one another without the fear of being policed, even if in a non-sexual way. Wherever I look in queer culture, swimming crops up as a seminal topic and point of reference. There are literary works like Alan Hollinghurst's *Swimming-Pool Library*, which explores in detail the male form, cruising and a private swimming pool in London. More recently, in *Swimming in the Dark*, Tomasz Jedrowski writes in beautiful prose about an intimate, gay-longing love affair between two men on summer camp in Poland in 1980. Their love is illegal and punishable, but they find closeness during their trips to the beach and in swimming together. In art, too, David Hockney is famous for his obsession with swimming pools. I don't think it's just because of their glistening, inviting reflections, California light or range of bluey-greeny colours, which he cites as inspiration when asked. His *Portrait of an Artist (Pool with Two Figures)*, which shows a fully clothed man looking onto a swimmer beneath the water, is the most expensive work by a living artist ever sold. There's an intimacy and curiosity between the figures that I think speaks to queer people in a way often missed by a straight gaze.

In New York, a gay subculture emerged in the 1970s on the piers by the waterfront. The piers were gateways where ships would rock up and goods were handled, so there were lots of people coming and going. Gay men would sunbathe and socialize, often nude, by the piers and the deteriorating architecture lent itself well to creating shadowy areas to cruise and have sex. Photos both from Peter Hujar and David Wojnarowicz show all kinds of illicit and homoerotic art from inside the crumbling warehouses on Pier 46, including an early artwork from Keith Haring. Tress, a homosexual man who used to frequent the piers and cruise for sex, said in an interview with historian Jonathan Weinberg, 'I could be light under the sunlight. Feeling the warmth on my head, on my face, letting him feel that and all the world... It was exhilaration and freedom finally."[1] The piers then, were the foundations of liberation, bringing homosexuality out of the shadows and into the streets, allowing pleasure to be experienced rather than denied or take place in secret. I think this notion speaks for many gay artists who have been working under such heavy policing of sexuality. They are able to explore sensual and intimate moments between men and show beautiful bodies of the male form in a way that is acceptable to wider society. I'm thinking here especially of the work of Henry Scott Tuke, whose homosexuality cannot be confirmed as he never came out while he was alive – he couldn't – but his oils of male bodies beside the beach and on boats in Cornwall certainly suggest a homoerotic gaze.

Hydro-eroticism then, seems to have its place firmly in queer culture, which I still think is present. While we still live in a society where growing up as gay is seen as a phase, homophobia and persecution still exist, there is solace and joy to be found in and around the water. Since realizing the history and connection between gay men and the water, I've made more of an effort to become comfortable in the water and with my own body. It feels as though I'm reconnecting with my heritage and the people who have, like me, tried to find joy in everyday experiences. I figured that if swimming can be a source of strength and part of the gay revolution, then maybe it can be part of mine too. And so, I have begun my own journey to reclaiming swimming and the ponds as a space for my trans gay body.

---

1   Weinberg, J. (2019) *Pier Groups*. University Park, PA: The Pennsylvania State University Press. p.148.

Dating

My new-found confidence in my body since swimming more regularly gave me a bit of joie de vivre. After a few successful hook-ups, I was starting to feel as though I possibly could do this – be gay, trans and happy. I could do all the things they said I couldn't – be comfortable in my own skin and find others who might find me attractive enough to date. I feel like the two went together, as they often do for everyone: the more confident you are, the more attractive you feel and become.

After a period of browsing Grindr and eventually getting bored of the same profiles and grid, I decided it was time to start dating and meeting boys for something more meaningful than a quick shag. I didn't put much pressure on it; I wasn't looking for my next five-year relationship or anything, especially since I had just started to find my feet since the last one. But I thought meeting a boy for something romantic would be nice.

I downloaded OkCupid and Chappy.

Usually the conversations would go something like this:

Hey!

Hey how're you

Great, you?

Yeah good - just chilling

Cool. What are you up to?

I mean, fucking hell. Larry Kramer, in his exceptionally poignant and powerful 1985 play *The Normal Heart*, writes that gay people belong to a culture of brave, miraculous men like Proust, Michelangelo, James Baldwin, Christopher Isherwood, Walt Whitman, Tennessee Williams...and this is the kind of tantalizing chat we give each other. Thrilling.

Admittedly, my dating life was less successful than my sex life. As a general rule, finding someone to have sex with was okay. We'd exchange a few messages, a few pictures, have a couple of days of chat, commit an hour or so to each other and then be off. Dating, as it turned out, was much harder.

* * *

I'd met this guy once before. Peter, he was called. Or maybe it was Marcus. Anyway, we'd met at a bar near White City, just outside the BBC building. It had been a lunch date and he'd ordered Champagne. I felt compelled to follow, even though I've never been bougie enough to order a glass of Champagne at a bar in my life. Soon enough we'd got pissed. He was into amateur musical theatre, so obviously I felt like

I'd met the love of my life, so I offered to pay the bill. In fact, I hadn't offered – I paid it while he was in the loo, because I thought that was more romantic. I think he agreed to date two because he felt guilty, and I lived on rice and beans for the next week.

Dating lesson #1: never pay the whole bill on a first date. Split it.

Our second date was his idea. Since we both liked theatre, it made sense for us to go and see a play. He got tickets as a member of this mystery shopper website – tickets were given for free in exchange for giving an honest, anonymous review of how the service was, how clean the theatre was, what the show was like, if the ushers told people to turn their phones off enough. That type of thing. I should have known then how this would go.

We met at a pub near the Tube station before the show and had a couple of drinks. He insisted on paying, which I appreciated since I was still living the rice and beans lifestyle. We talked about his work and his housemate, who was doing some tinkering with the boiler. Or maybe they weren't doing something with the boiler. Maybe he wanted them to do something with the boiler. Anyway, it was something with a boiler. I talked about my job and a couple of the books I'd been reading recently and showed him the Instagram account of a new shop I'd found that did the most gorgeous patterned kitchen tiles. He was as interested as you think he was.

Before heading to the theatre, I went to the bathroom. I thought the toilets at the pub would be less crowded. As I entered, a stench caught my nostrils and I noticed the stall no longer had a door on it. That's the one thing I miss about women's toilets: there are always stalls with doors and they're *so* much cleaner. No piss on the floor or toilet seat. I decided to leave it, choosing instead to rest on a full bladder rather than straddling a piss-ridden toilet seat and humiliating myself in a doorless cubicle.

It turned out that the play started at 7 p.m., and not 7:30, as Peter had thought. We arrived just in time to join the queue into the auditorium.

The play was set in the round, so there were audience seats circling the entirety of the tiny stage. In the middle was a make-up desk and mirror with a single seat, lit in red. Suddenly it struck me that I had no idea what we were about to see. I hadn't even thought about it. I'd just stupidly and absent-mindedly said yes.

Dating lesson #2: know what it is you're actually going to do/see.

The lights went down, silence filled the auditorium and the play began.

Even though I saw the play, I'm not sure I could describe what it was, who it was for, or why it happened. I'm not sure the cast could either. It was a mess. Think your worst-nightmare GCSE drama assessment type of thing. I was so distracted by the absurdity of what was happening on stage – actors rolling around on the floor with what I assume was meant to be dramatic lighting but one of the bulbs had gone – that I'd for a time forgotten about my needing to pee. I turned to Peter next to me and said that I'd be back. I crept next to the stage during the next available blackout, hoping not to bump into any of the cast members standing dramatically off the stage. I found the toilet and stayed in there longer than I needed to, wondering when the interval might come.

When I really couldn't prolong returning any longer, I made my way back to the theatre. I stopped at the door, which had an usher guarding it. Without a word, he pointed at a sign said, 'NO INTERVAL. NO READMITTANCE'.

Fuck. 'I just really needed the toilet,' I pleaded.

He shoved his forefinger at the sign again.

'I know, I'm sorry to be rude, but my bag's in there and so is my friend...'

And so is my wine, I remembered.

He muttered something about a blackout and a patron into his radio.

I waited for two minutes, hoping my bladder wouldn't fill up again before the end of the show now that I'd broken the seal and I'd have to leave *again*.

After what felt like forever of awkward no-talking and usher-glaring, they escorted me into the theatre during a period of darkness and sat me on one of the (many) empty seats, directly opposite where I was sat before. Peter looked incredulous and confused. He beckoned me over with a quizzical, bemused look on his face, while the actors were in the middle of a slow-motion fight sequence. I looked at the usher to see if I could risk it, but they eyed me carefully.

For the remainder of the show, I sat opposite my date, suffering the insufferable, cringing at my own awkwardness.

Eventually and thankfully, the show ended and the lights were raised in the auditorium as people were leaving. I felt them pile past me as I waited for Peter to make his way across to meet me. There was an uncomfortable, awkward silence between us which I tried to break by asking, 'Do you fancy a drink? A wine in the bar maybe?' A beat. 'No, I think I'll get back,' he replied casually. At the entranceway as couples and friends folded into the night, we gave each other a distant, cumbersome hug before making our separate ways to the Tube.

The next day, when I hadn't heard from him, I messaged:

> Hey, how're you? Thanks for last night.

No reply.

I decided to turn my phone onto aeroplane mode for three hours so that when I'd turn it back on, he'd probably have messaged back.

Still nothing.

I messaged again:

> I hope the interviews aren't going too bad at work today?

Nothing.
Until:

> Hey! Good thanks. It was nice meeting you but I don't think I really felt that spark. I'm sure you'll find someone soon.

> Also you were a bit embarrassing at the theatre.

My first proper gay date and it had been a disaster. All that effort, time and money spent on a couple of dates – the getting excited, picking out outfits, staying for the remainder of terrible plays. All for nothing. Not even holding hands or a kiss. Obviously, I'd already thought I'd fallen for him, and I thought I'd never find anyone to date ever again. It was the first time I'd ever received that 'Look, I don't think it's working out' text. Little did I know there were dozens still to come.

* * *

Thankfully, it only took me a few days to get over the 'I don't think it's quite working out'. Not at all like the long, arduous months spent pining after Lucy. I desperately want not to feel hurt and rejected again, so I found the best way to get over it was to quickly move on to someone else. Fill the sadness with longing and hope for a new boy. Be distracted. Swipe right until the swipes had run out. That kind of thing. The goal, I told myself, was that every time I picked up my phone there would be a notification from a boy. That's when I'd feel wanted. That's when I'd feel accepted by gay men. And if there wasn't a notification, I'd just need to try harder.

Talking to boys, flirting and meeting up for the odd date and hook-up was well and good until I started counting the hours until I could swipe again. I began refreshing Grindr every time I was somewhere new in the hope of catching someone in my geographical net I hadn't seen before. My increased sex and dating app usage was propelled by a fear of rejection, although I didn't realize this at the time. I needed as many boys on the go at once as possible so if one fizzled out or sent the classic 'I don't think it's working' text, I could bounce back quickly. It was a way of protecting and distracting myself. An endless carousel of men and spreading my options as widely as I could was my safety barrier. It was a way to keep myself from feeling any more hurt. And so I started to check Grindr at breakfast, during lunch time, on loo breaks, when meeting for coffee with friends. It became addictive. I was always looking for the next man, completely ignoring the people and opportunities I already had in front of me.

My diary, previously free of a sex and love life and void of intimacy after Lucy and I broke up, became full again. On average it was four dates a week, slotted between work, hook-ups and swimming. I began writing brief outlines of the dates and boys I met in my Google Calendar on my way home so I could refresh my memory if we met again. It was difficult, expensive and exhausting to try to keep up with my own schedule.

It felt as though I was beginning to spiral. Although I'd come out as gay and was starting to enjoy the opportunities this new gay freedom offered, I felt I was beginning to lose myself as well. There is an irony that coming out brings – we come out and are 'our true selves' whilst simultaneously trying to fit into a crowd. I thought that being gay was about going out and having sex and meeting as many boys as possible, so I put a lot of pressure on myself to do that. To fit in. Over a few months, my social life had become more like a serial-dating life, really. And when I say dating, I mean a real mix of going out for dinner and drinks and just hooking up with people I'd chatted to briefly on Grindr. I spent all my free time and evenings searching, searching, searching – Lord knows what for, something, someone, I suppose, to spend my evenings with so I didn't feel lonely.

I think I slept with most people in my vicinity, because it got to the point where I had to create narrower filters to find faces (or torsos) on Grindr I hadn't come across before. I say slept with, but this didn't mean they spent the night. In fact, I preferred they didn't. Mostly it was about getting them in and out as quickly as possible – strange, considering I spent so much energy finding them in the first place.

Spending an evening alone almost felt like I'd failed myself and I'd been rejected. And being rejected was the worst thing I could possibly imagine. If nobody wanted to have sex with me, I felt like I was unattractive and therefore valueless as a person. I told myself that it made sense to keep searching for sex, no matter who with, while I was looking for a boyfriend because that's what being gay was about – sexual liberation. Gay men, I told myself, were warriors of sexual freedom. After all, our magazines were full of porn, saunas and fetish gear, so I told myself that I was just doing the same as everyone else. I didn't realize then that I'd fallen into what I can only describe as an addictive cycle, trying to find men and sex in order to find something resembling worth and happiness. My whole value as a person was completely dependent on how fuckable I was to other gay men.

I started to realize that I had a problem when I noticed that I was online more time than I was off. From the sample of boys listed on my 'favourites', I could see some of them had been offline for several days, only loading the app when they felt interested or horny, but here I was on a constant search for 'fun'. That word had started to define and dictate my existence. If I wasn't having 'fun', I was worthless and redundant. I was constantly looking for fun, having fun, advertising for fun, begging for fun...until it felt anything but.

It wasn't even like I was horny all the time either. I wasn't actually wanting or craving sex. I wasn't craving intimacy or an orgasm. What I wanted was other people – men – to want and need me. I wanted to be seen and accepted by gay men as one of them. And because so much of gay culture is dependent on sex and there is value in youth and fuckability, I thought I needed to use my body as a way to find acceptance.

I think it started with shame. I learned from my earliest memories that to be lesbian, gay, bisexual, trans and queer was to be inherently flawed, unlovable and valueless to society. That we are innately wrong. Don't play with those toys, be polite, be pretty, wear that dress, cross your legs when sitting down, have your hair down and wear it long, like Barbies, don't play with boys' toys... Subconsciously I absorbed the message that what came so naturally to me was wrong. So the shame became deep rooted and grew bigger from within me. I encouraged men to thrust into me so I could feel something...something that might resemble acceptance. This drive to feel accepted, loved, appreciated and valued in the guise of 'fun' and sex started to become not at all fun, and it got me into some really dangerous situations.

At times it was out of control. I met up with guys not even knowing their names or how old they were or without telling anyone where I was. One time, a guy wouldn't let me leave his house until my friend texted me and I made a frantic 'Sorry I have to meet my friend' escape. I felt so ashamed of myself and that I allowed myself to get into that situation that I sought comfort in other men. I knew it was terrible for me. The cycle became additive and toxic. I felt shame so I sought sex, and then I felt shame about the sex, so I sought comfort and acceptance from someone else. Somewhere along the way I'd learned that the answer to shame and acceptance was sex. I'd internalized so much negativity about myself and believed that I was wrong, that being fucked was the only way to be right.

My Knight in a Shining Jockstrap

I always look up while walking around Soho. The buildings are tall, sandwiched together like odd pieces of a jigsaw puzzle, and despite living here since I was 18, I always spot something I've never seen before. Just recently, it was the blue English Heritage plaque of Karl Marx, who, apparently, lived on Dean Street for five years. He wrote his first novel, *Das Kapital*, there. The plaque sits above a restaurant and bakery, one of the many I'm still yet to step foot in.

Sometime after my disastrous date, I wandered down Dean Street, eyes aloft, and I could almost feel Soho's history pouring through the windows and brickwork onto the street. It was as if history was snaking through the cracks in the concrete, up through my toes, through my trunk, surrounding me in a close embrace. You may think that sounds dramatic and eccentric (you'd be right), but Soho does make me feel like I'm surrounded by the past. There are few places I feel like that – where history holds me. Since my breakup and attempts at embracing a single life and becoming more comfortable with gayness, I've felt closer to Soho. I think it's because, as queer people, we are too often robbed of our ancestors, whose sexuality has either been rewritten or left out of history books entirely. But in Soho there is rich, known and accessible queer history. There is a sense of belonging.

As I walk, I think of the 18th-century molly houses, which investigative journalist Ned Ward (first published in 1709) describes as a meeting place for a 'Gang of Sodomitical Wretches' and for people who 'are so far degenerated from all masculine Deportment, or manly Exercises, that they rather fancy themselves Women'.[1] I'd found this out in an online queer history class by the Bishopsgate Institute. Molly houses, I learned, were the forefathers (or foreparents) to what we now know as gay bars. Of course, due to their illegality, they weren't advertised as such, but knowledge of them spread quickly between those 'in the know'. And they could have been anywhere – in a brandy shop, a coffee house, a theatre bar – wherever they were, dozens of men would meet for sex, for love, for stage performances sometimes incorporating drag, for 'marriage' ceremonies. They offered a safe space for gay people to discuss their identities and socialize with other homosexuals, much like we do in queer spaces now. I thought about the changing landscape of queerness of Soho, how the names and places of queer spaces may have changed over time but the need for them remained the same – a need to meet, socialize, have sex and fall in and out of love with other people like us. Yes, being gay in the UK now may not be the same long, dark walk to the gallows if anyone finds out our secret, but undoubtedly we are still othered, we

---

1   Norton, R. (1999) 'The Mollies Club, 1709–1710.' In *Homosexuality in Eighteenth-Century England: A Sourcebook*. Accessed on 21/09/2022 at www. rictornorton.co.uk/eighteen/nedward.htm

continue to be the victims of homophobic and transphobic hate crimes and discrimination and still suffer alienation from our families. Our outsider status is the beating heart of our experience as queer people. It is only in gay spaces that our otherness isn't so 'other' and our 'nature' is celebrated rather than shamed.

I continued my wander along Dean Street and was reminded of the artist John Minton and his friends who drank ravenously in the Colony Room of number 41 Dean Street, only a few feet from where I was walking. John Minton, Lucian Freud, Francis Bacon, Keith Vaughan and The Two Roberts (Colquhoun and MacBryde) were a circle of artists in the 19th century who I consider to be some of the 'greats' and whose work offers me immense comfort. They were queer artists who painted, drew, drank and made love to their friends and each other before going back to their studios and repeating the process. Their friendships and love affairs fuelled their work and, as homosexuality was desperately illegal, Soho allowed them a space to be. It was their bohemian utopia. A steaming epicentre of creativity, art and queerness. They thought of the art world and Soho as a sort of demimonde, where usual societal rules didn't seem to apply. Their work, particularly that of Keith Vaughan's, captures illicit love at a time when their love and lust was unlawful. I feel a beauty, joy and yearning sadness in his art. I've studied their work, characters and relationships for years, and viewing Keith Vaughan's endless drawings of male nudes by the ponds was somewhat of a gay awakening for me. Feeling close to this history and a connection with the characters within it is one of the many reasons I regularly visit Hampstead Heath ponds. I thought of *their Soho* and what the place might have meant to them. A place to escape to, most likely, to find their peers, their lovers and inspiration for their work. Not so dissimilar to how I feel about Soho.

I don't pretend that Soho's all rosy. It has history and character, certainly, perhaps even charm, but I imagine it was a hard place to be, scary and dangerous. Soho's queer culture was born not out of choice but out of desperation. To have a place for people who had been 'othered' and marginalized by mainstream society. Soho can be a cruel mistress and can have a sting in her tail if you're not careful. The molly houses in Soho, as enticing as they may sound, were regularly raided and invaded by petty police attempting to incite and arrest. And Soho for Minton, Vaughan and friends was lustful, yes, but beauteous and kind, never. For me, I've had nights where I've been spat at in the street and been pushed into oncoming traffic when leaving gay bars in Soho. This is a reminder that even in places where seemingly we are free to be ourselves, there is still a requirement to be on guard.

Soho, despite having the largest cluster of gay bars in London, is not a queer haven. Like many place the lure of 'otherness' and bohemia has attracted tourists to gawp and gasp at what little queer culture there is left. I need more than two hands to count the number of times I've witnessed visitors snigger and point at our flags, tease and stare open-mouthed at our sex shops. Capitalism and gentrification has pushed authentic queer venues out to the East End, Clapham and Vauxhall. This is not, as some may argue, because they're not needed or because being gay is more acceptable than it once was, or because 'we have Grindr so nobody needs these spaces to meet any more'. It's because venues are facing rocketing rental rates, lack of protection, gentrification and redevelopment. In the past few years we have lost over

60 per cent of our queer bars and this is a desperate tragedy.[2] We are losing our history and our homes.

But there is hope. Queer people are doing what they do best: organizing in the face of struggle. While physical meeting places are shrinking, community spaces and specialist club nights are emerging. The London LGBTQ+ Community Centre opened its doors in 2021 and initially came about as a pop-up centre in response to isolation and loneliness during the Covid-19 pandemic. UK Black Pride is now the world's largest celebration for African, Asian, Middle Eastern, Latin American and Caribbean heritage LGBTQIA+ people. It's been incredible to witness its growth and momentum since I first visited supporting a newly out friend back in 2018. Opening Doors provides spaces and community groups for LGBTQIA+ people around the UK who are over 50. It has become clear that although we're losing queer spaces in a literal bricks and mortar sense, our community organizing, club nights and groups are thriving in London. The need now is to push this further afield and try to support our queer family in remote places who may not have access to spaces where they can be themselves.

* * *

Finally, I reached my destination: Clone Zone. I paused. Its entrance is uncompromising, and the glass windows aren't afraid to bare all. Two mannequins with vibrant green and pink jockstraps guard the entrance as a television screen

---

2   Kheraj, A. (2021) *Queer London: A Guide to the City's LGBTQ+ Past and Present*. Woodbridge: ACC Art Books. p.6.

flicks to images of half-naked, sculpted torsos and fine peachy arses perched on car bonnets parked in the desert. Queerness in Soho no longer hides in nondescript molly houses or in secret above Soho's watering holes. Gayness, including its culture and kink, is out, loud and unapologetic. That is not to say it is accepted by everyone, but the fact we have sex shops for gay men on the street for anyone to walk into, and they're not hidden or disguised as 'bookshops' (as many sex shops in Soho used to be), is a significant step forward. I find power in the fact that they stand strong, resistant and resilient, refusing to lurk in the shadows. The fact that this shop is allowed a premises or lease at all is a far cry from the days of molly houses or Minton and his friends. This is something they could only ever dream of.

I paused, anxious that strangers would notice I was walking in. But more than that, I was nervous about the shop itself. I had imagined what it might be like inside, but I didn't fully know what to expect, or indeed what I was looking for or looking at. When I entered, my eyes moved from jockstraps to socks to poppers to harnesses to lube to facemasks to the signs leading downstairs to what I could only assume was raunchier fetish gear. It felt unfamiliar and new.

Despite being a gay man, and this being a shop for people like me, I felt a bit like an outsider looking in. Of course, I had seen and gawked open-mouthed at pictures of handsome men in harnesses, jockstraps and other kink paraphernalia – I wasn't a complete newbie – but I'd never considered that wearing these things was an option for me. I wanted to give myself the opportunity to see if I was wrong.

As a girl, sexy underwear meant lacy bras or the occasional red thong. Harnesses, pup masks, full-length rubber suits, leather harnesses and hoods, though, were entirely something else. I knew I didn't have to be into all this stuff. Fetish and underwear such as jockstraps, sexy briefs, thongs, etc. aren't for everyone and not all gay men are into them. But I wanted to experiment and see. I wanted to challenge myself to not be afraid to enter spaces because of my transness.

A friendly, kind-eyed man welcomed me into the shop, letting me know he was there if I had any questions. I had hundreds of questions, thousands...but none came to me. My mind fell completely blank. I browsed the shop, ogling at harnesses, mesh tops, leather straps and more variation in men's underwear than I had ever seen before. Jockstraps were stacked upon each other like cards in a gift shop – ones with thin elastic waists, thick elastic waists, different thicknesses and materials at the front and lack of material at the back. I spun the metal rack round until I found one I liked. It had a blue bulge with a thin black-and-white waistline and two black straps that would sit underneath my bum cheeks. I looked at the sizes. Small and medium looked tiny. I looked at the underwear, down at my body, and back to the jocks. I usually wore a small, but there was no way my body was going to fit into those. I have an hourglass figure and the widest part of my body is my waist, not my shoulders, as a cis man's would be. I picked up a large pair, the ones I thought my hips would fit into comfortably, and paid at the counter.

I tried the jockstrap on at home without turning to face the mirror. The relationship I have with my own reflection can be strained, and so I have learned to put on clothes facing away from my reflection. I stepped into the elastic holes – one for each leg – and pulled them up to my groin so the elastic fit comfortably around the crease of each cheek. The open window let in a small breeze and I felt a brush of cold against my cheeks. I was made all too aware of the lack of fabric. I felt exposed. Naked. Vulnerable. I suppose that's the appeal, isn't it? I noticed I wasn't completely averse to letting myself feel vulnerable.

The point of jockstraps isn't just to look at pert bums. It makes it easier and sexier for men to have anal sex. At that time, I hadn't had anal sex before. I was worried about it. I told myself that I didn't need to have anal sex; I could use my pussy instead. It was relaxed, it self-lubricated, it didn't need douching or forward planning, there's more intense sensation. Standing in my jockstrap now, exposed, I sensed the returning, repetitive negative questioning of whether I was gay enough. If I wasn't having anal sex, was I missing a fundamental part of being gay? Did it matter? I knew rationally that choosing to have anal sex or not doesn't make a person any less or any more of a gay man – regardless of whether they are cis or trans. But I couldn't shake this question of enoughness. A large part of this for me is because the rhetoric and dialogue about gay men when I was growing up focused so much on anal sex. 'Bumming' was something only gay men did. It's what made them different. Gay sex, seemingly, was and could only be anal sex.

I moved my hands from underneath the elastic bands sitting at the bottom of my cheeks to my front, where the pronounced bulge lay empty. I could feel the excess blue fabric at the front, an empty pocket, clearly designed to house and accentuate my penis, which was not there. Unfulfilled space. I pulled at it, feeling the empty fabric on my fingertips, and was left with a pang of longing for hanging flesh that would never belong to me, wishing for my body to naturally fill the space. I inhaled a deep breath and counted to five as I breathed out. These are regular thoughts for me, and in the past I would have panicked, taken off the clothes and vowed never to wear them again. And when it got really bad, I'd cancel my plans and not leave my bedroom. Except this happens far too regularly – in fancy underwear or not – for never leaving my bedroom to be an option. I have work to go to, family to see, a life to live. So I have learned to confront these feelings with deep breathing techniques and allow the thoughts to come into my head and wash over me. I have to give myself compassion and time and remember that I am a trans person living in a cis world. It takes a great deal of mental control and effort to steady my body and tell myself that I am not lacking or wrong. That I do not have to cut off parts of my body or stick new bits on to be seen as 'fixed', because my trans body was never broken in the first place.

I turned to face the mirror in my new jockstrap, fearing my own reflection. To my own surprise, I was encouraged by what I saw. I thought I would see myself in underwear that clearly didn't fit, baggy in some places, too tight in others, looking alien in my own skin. But I didn't. My cheeks arched well and the straps beneath supported them a little, framing my arse as if it was the centrepiece. And the cloth at the front didn't stick out or look lacking at all; it moulded its way, admittedly with a little bump, around my body. I placed my thumb under the straps at the back and toyed with them a while, spinning and turning to see myself in this new light. I let my hands wander around my strong arms, my flat, hairy chest, my curved arse and my muscular thighs. I allowed myself to connect with my body and the person looking back at me. I felt proud of the gay man I saw in front of me. Proud of the courage it took to go into the shop, to try something new and face fear. It's then I realized that I'd become the man of my own dreams. The man I'd always wanted and imagined myself to be.

My own knight in a shining jockstrap.

It is one of my proudest accomplishments to be able to read my own reflection of me and enjoy what I see. Because I had spent 18 years feeling like I didn't belong in myself, and although my body has always been my own, the body I now live in is new and it still takes some getting used to. My flat, designer chest is sculpted by a surgeon, my fat is redistributed by testosterone and that same testosterone makes hair sprout in unwanted places. This is not the body that I was born with; it has been made, created, sculpted. It is intentional. It is magic.

I turned to face my front in the mirror. I looked down towards my hips and the fabric, which I had felt was lacking earlier, and enjoyed seeing my queer body staring back at me in full form. I felt whole. I felt powerful. I felt sexy. The mirror showed me the body – the person – I'd worked so hard to be. Scars an' all.

Sauna

The first time I went to a gay sauna was at four o'clock on a Sunday morning in mid-November. It was freezing and I was really sad. You know that kind of post-night out, I've had too much to drink and I want to text all my exes type sad? Exactly that.

The night had started off alright. I'd been out dancing at the RVT (again – classic me), but now my friends had gone home and I was left to make my way back to West London, alone. I wasn't in a good place. I'd drunk too much, messaged too many boys and genuinely felt quite lost. I was losing control of myself – my job, my money, my health. So I had gone drinking and dancing to try to feel better. I wanted to feel closer to the gay community and feel the joy other gay men seemed to have. The flair, the glitter, the camp, the happy. It had worked for a few hours. I'd danced to Robyn and flirted my way across the dance floor. Everyone seemed to like me when I was happy, care-free Harry. They said they liked me when I was drunk. When I let my hair down and I was the life and soul of the party. But now my friends had gone – they had brunch plans for tomorrow, apparently, so I was left to find my own way home.

Somehow I'd managed to get on the wrong bus home. Rather than taking me in the direction of Oxford Circus, I'd gone to Waterloo. Fuck knows how I was going to get back from there. It was getting really late, and I shuddered. Three degrees. I checked Uber. Seventy pounds for a taxi home. Fuckedy fuck fuuuuuck.

It turns out the Tesco near Waterloo station is open 24 hours, although there's not much stock at that time. In fact, there's only limp chicken-mayo wraps, which is what I had. I purchased it at the self-checkout, watching the mirror image of my face in the screen as I paid. It was like that moment when babies look at themselves in the mirror for the first time. They're confused. They don't know if it's themselves they're looking at or someone else. I felt like that too. My eyes rolled back.

I sat outside on the ground, knees bent and shivering, taking bites into a red-coloured wrap filled with strings of lettuce. Unsurprisingly, it didn't do much to sober me up.

I had at least two and a half hours until the Tube would start running again, and I had time to kill. I knew there was a gay sauna around Waterloo. I'd read about it in one of those free gay-scene-what's-on-in-London-type magazines you get in Gay's the Word. I didn't know much about saunas other than they were all a bit anonymous, a lot of sex took place and they're for gay men only. I didn't know if they'd allow trans men in. But I am curious by nature, and I like a challenge. Plus, I wasn't sober enough to care. I searched for the name of it on my phone. Pleasuredrome. I punched it into Google Maps and did my best I'm-not-drunk-stagger all the way there.

The sauna entrance is hidden. It's just underneath the

arches and if you aren't looking for it, you'd walk past it entirely. I opened the door and entered.

* * *

A friendly faced man stood at the counter, thumbing something into a keyboard. I could see he was watching me carefully, assessing how drunk I was.

I composed my best sober face.

There was a stack of towels behind him, and a card reader was sitting on the counter.

'Just one please.' I think that's what people who go to saunas would say.

I thought I remembered something in the magazine about under 25s getting in cheaper. I'm sure that's what it said. Or maybe that was somewhere else.

I showed my ID. 'Under 25.'

He nodded, handed me the card reader and I offered my card to pay.

Moments later I stood in a maze of floor-to-ceiling lockers with a wristband key and towel. There were men everywhere, clothed, unclothed, towels, no towels. I didn't know where to look. I searched for my locker number, which took much longer than it should have done, and got changed.

I was nervous now. I didn't know what I was thinking. I could feel the heat from the sauna room filling the changing area, and suddenly I was really thirsty. I touched the roof of my mouth with my tongue: dry. I slowly undressed, looking around me to see if anyone was watching. Nobody was. I imagine all the looking was going on inside the sauna itself. I decided to keep my boxers on underneath my white towel – not the done thing – but it made me feel more secure.

Inside, it wasn't what I expected. I'd imagined red lights in a dark, cramped space, full of sweat and the sounds of men moaning. In reality, I'd walked into a space that looked like a friendly bar where men stood in their towels, chatting to each other over a beer or coffee. I overheard a conversation between two men. One said he worked in finance, while the other replied that he was a performer. His body could have told me that much. I sat thinking about the strange charm-ness of it all. I had imagined a place like a sauna to be really cold (not in heat, obviously, but in vibe) but I found the opposite. Here were two men, from completely different careers, having (probably) never met before having a casual chat just as they would if they had just met on the bus or at a coffee shop. I found it rather endearing, almost sweet. I stood at the counter and asked for a glass of water, trying to settle in and relax, trying to take the place in.

I'm in now, I might as well make the most of it, I thought.

To the left of the bar was a small jacuzzi area, where another couple of guys were hanging out. Opposite on the warm sun loungers were three larger men, all fast asleep, snoring loudly. I crept past them, finding the courage to go for a wander.

One of the first things I saw was the porn. It was playing on a large screen with no sound. A large, muscular, hairless man fucked an equally muscley and hairless man beneath him. They weren't my type and apparently nor was it the type of the guy in the cinema room, as he lay on his back, towel on the floor, fast asleep. I left him to it.

I found a set of stairs, and red halogen lights cast eery shadows up the steps. This was it. This was more what I had imagined. I composed myself, filling my chest with air, just as I did at the ponds, to give myself a more muscular frame. I put one foot in front of the other and made my way upstairs.

Here, at least the men were awake. They wandered, seemingly in circles, keeping their eyes open for new trade. The doors in the middle remained closed. The noise of men fucking and men being fucked permeated through the walls. Soft exhales, harsher grunts. I continued to walk round, resting on the wall occasionally, imitating the guys I'd seen. I kept my hands clenched firmly around my towel, noticing how sweaty my hands had become.

Eventually I grew bored of looking. And tired. And really, *really* thirsty.

As I made my way back downstairs, I began to realize just how hot it had been and how dehydrated I was. I grabbed another drink of water from the bar. That's when I noticed the television. They were playing *BBC News*, and it was now 5:30 in the morning. I perched in the nearest available alcove and watched the images flash across the screen.

Patchy showers and a chance of frost for much of the UK, the subtitles read. Highs of eight, lows of five, with rain moving from the south up to Scotland...

I looked in a daze at the screen, watching images flicker, through half-shut eyes.

* * *

As it turns out, gay saunas are a fairly decent place to wait for the first Tube of the morning. It's warm, they offer fresh towels and refreshments and they play non-stop *BBC News*. I didn't fuck or have any kind of action that night – I was far too tired, scared and uncertain of my surroundings – but on the upside, I was up to date with current affairs by the time I got home.

Leaving the sauna felt like a harsh push back into reality. There aren't any clocks in the sauna (television aside) and so I can understand how many gay men lose themselves completely in there. Walking to the Tube station, I saw people walking their dogs, on their runs, on their way to work. We were in the same place at the same time, but it felt like we were in separate spaces entirely. I got on the Tube, exhausted, and thought about my experience.

I was disappointed that I didn't feel brave enough to be fully naked underneath my towel, but I acknowledged that even drunk, I was trying to look after my own safety. I had my scars on show, so I clearly wasn't hiding my transness, but I still wasn't able to predict the response of gay men having a trans person there. I'd seen a *Attitude* article a while back reporting on a story that a gay sauna had kicked a gay trans man out on the basis that they only accepted 'biological males'.[1] I hadn't known if I would face a situation like that, too, but I didn't allow my trepidation or fear to restrain me from experiencing the things I wanted to.

As it turned out, the people in the sauna the night that I went didn't seem to care. If they were interested in me, they'd make that known by making a head gesture or moving closer, and if they weren't, they just walked on by. It was respectful in that sense. I wasn't looking for sex (being in the space was more than enough newness for me), so I didn't respond to any advances.

---

1   Attitude (2018) 'London Gay Sauna Kicks Out Trans Man for Not Having a Penis.' *Attitude*, 1 November, 2018. Accessed on 20/09/2022 at https://attitude.co.uk/article/london-gay-sauna-kicks-out-trans-man-for-not-having-a-penis-1/19517

I wished real life was more like it was in the sauna. Where people just walked on by, not caring if you're trans or not, and had the respect not to touch you if you didn't want them to. I felt strangely proud of myself on the Tube ride home. I felt proud that I'd allowed and encouraged myself to be in a space that is understandably terrifying for many trans people. But that I'd manged to push myself out of my comfort zone and be in a space which we've not always been allowed to be in. It was powerful. My very presence felt like I was disrupting typically cis male-only gay spaces.

Men Can't Get Pregnant

In and outside of saunas, sex has its challenges. I'm not only talking about not being able to get a hard-on, or a condom breaking, or any of the other things that people – cis and trans – face. I'm talking about the specific trans-related concerns around sex, which are all too often missed or simply not considered.

When I hook up with guys, we've always discussed what we both like to do in the bedroom, agreed rules and boundaries and discussed contraception and codewords, and he's *always* been fully aware of my transness before he comes round or I knock on his door. That's not because I feel that I owe my truth to anyone or that I feel like I'm being disingenuous if I don't say. It's just easier this way. Guys know what they're letting themselves in for.

I had started to hook up with a lot of guys. Too many to keep count of, really. I thought the more sex I had, the better I'd feel about my body, my sexuality and my manliness. But despite how many men I was hosting, the relationship I had with my body didn't get easier. I'd compare myself to men and give myself unreasonable aims regarding how I should look. Thinner, taller, bigger arms, thicker neck, bigger feet, fuller beard, more toned, less curved. I've since realized that there is no point comparing myself to a cis man's body. That is unreasonable; it's unattainable. But that doesn't mean it hurts any less.

I was thinking about all this as a guy called Elliot was fucking me. We'd met on Grindr a few days previously, and now I found myself with my legs wrapped around his waist as he pushed into me. My head looked up to the ceiling and I thought about how my body responded to him. I was aware of how my 'love handles' – the skin at either side of my hips – moved as he held on to them. We didn't kiss or say anything really. It was just one of those routine hook-ups. He was free, I had an evening to kill and I really didn't want to spend any time alone.

I don't know when the condom split. I don't know whether he realized and carried on or whether it was a genuine mistake. But he didn't seem very surprised when he eventually finished and took it off. He folded it awkwardly and put it on the bedside table.

I've never felt shame quite like I did sitting on the toilet pan, panic-pushing the cum of a man I barely knew out of my body. I felt stupid. How did I let this happen? How did I let myself get to a place where I was hurting and putting myself in danger meeting up with strangers because I couldn't stomach spending an evening on my own? Because I couldn't face the feeling I had when I was on my own. It was like I'd turned men into a numbers game. The more men I had sex with, the more of a gay man I was. And the more they wanted me, the more I felt validated in my identity. I felt so much shame.

I thought back to the shy boy who was nervous to be on apps and meet with anyone at all. I couldn't really fathom how I had managed to get here. I clenched and squeezed the last out of me, peeing, wiping and standing up. I washed my hands and looked in the mirror.

Who am I?

What am I *doing*?

As I tip-toed back into my bedroom I found him spread-eagle on my bed, still panting. He looked exhausted. I looked at him, suddenly feeling disgusted by sex and what we'd done.

'Are you okay? Do you want water before you head off?' I asked.

'Nooooo, just come here and cuddle.'

I didn't want to cuddle. But I also didn't want to be a dick. I rested my head on his chest.

'What are your plans for tonight?' I hinted again, more forcefully this time.

'Shhhhh, cuddling is the best bit. I'm not one of those guys who just leaves.'

Ha. Typical. All I had wanted was for someone to stay, and now all I wanted was for him to go. And now he wouldn't bloody leave.

'Well, I'm going out for dinner with some friends tonight and I've got to shower,' I lied.

'Oh, okay.' He looked disappointed.

'Yeah...sorry.'

Eventually he got up, leaving a large sweat mark on my bedsheet. I followed, finding my feet, and hovered near my bedroom door, hoping he would hurry up. He was half-dressed and about to pull on his T-shirt when he tried to give me another kiss, pushing his tongue down my throat. I moved my lips away, offering my cheek instead.

'See you again,' I said, closing the door and pulling away.

Early the next morning, after I'd changed my sheets, I went straight to the pharmacy. I knew I needed to get the morning-after pill. I'd hardly slept and had woken up in panic at intervals throughout the night. When I first started taking testosterone, the doctors told me that it would make me infertile. I had to sign a document at 18 to say I understood this. It turns out that this wasn't accurate as little to no research had ever really been done on the topic. It was just an assumption. Trans men have gotten and do get pregnant. If they want to have a child, they come off testosterone because it may potentially harm the unborn child, not because testosterone works as some kind of miracle contraceptive.

I roped my flatmate into coming along with me for extra support. We got dressed and walked to the pharmacy, not saying very much. I felt ashamed and scared. I didn't want to explain to Elliot that the condom broke and I'd need medication. I doubt he'd ever really considered that I could get pregnant. It's often a thing gay men say, isn't it? – 'We can have all the sex we want and not worry about pregnancy.' Well, not in this case. Thinking about that made me feel isolated again. Like I was the only guy who had to do this.

I asked my flatmate if he'd go into the pharmacy for me. I assumed that guys went in for their girlfriends all the time.

'Sure!' he said, offering a supportive smile.

I watched as he opened the door, walked in and began speaking to the pharmacist.

Relief.

'That was quick!' I said as he returned. Then I noticed he was empty handed.

'They wouldn't give it to me. You need to go in yourself.'

I sighed heavily and closed my eyes, psyching myself up and finding the courage from I don't know where.

I walked slowly towards the automatic doors and past an older man reading the detail on the back of a box for toe plasters and stood at the counter. I pulled what little confidence I had from within me. 'I'd like the morning-after pill, please.'

The woman behind the counter looked at me, puzzled. And then an almost exasperated run-off-her-feet look appeared on her face.

'No, your mate's just come in. I've explained to him already. She'll have to come in herself.'

A beat. My face began to redden. I could feel it starting to burn.

'No. It's for me,' I said, trying to stay as matter-of-fact as I could.

A smile began to draw on her face. 'What do you mean?'

'It's for me,' I repeated, looking around to see if anyone else was listening.

The older guy was still examining the toe plasters. What more information could he possibly need? They're plasters for *toes*.

'Boys can't get pregnant. If she's worried, she'll need to come in herself and then we can have a chat.' She'd started to get defensive. She probably thought I was taking the piss or was a time waster or something.

I already felt exhausted.

I lifted my hands and widened my arms, in an I-don't-know-what-to-tell-you kind of way.

'I'm a trans man. The morning after pill is for me,' I repeated again, exasperated now.

She studied me. She seemed confused. I could see her brain working. She didn't know what to do. She probably hadn't had a training course for this. She looked at her colleague, who remained very still and didn't care to look up or get involved.

She looked suspicious, then signalled to a booth on my right. 'Shall we go in here?'

It was a grey plastic square booth. Oversized for such a small pharmacy. I noticed there was no ceiling to it. I'm not sure what kind of privacy it would actually give.

I complied, not saying anything more.

We sat opposite each other. Me on one of those blue padded chairs with metal legs. Her, opposite, with a computer, keyboard and desk between us. I was grateful for the separation. It made me feel safer.

She looked at me, as if to say, 'Explain then.'

'I'm a trans man, I had sex yesterday and the condom split. I take testosterone, which is why I look like this.' I gestured to my receding hairline and fully grown beard. 'The testosterone stops my periods, but I can still get pregnant. You can check my medical records if you don't believe me.'

Without a second thought, she reached for the keyboard, 'Name?' I couldn't believe we were actually doing this. 'Harry' I said, my face burning with both anger and embarrassment.

She clicked her mouse and scanned the screen, presumably looking at my seven-odd years' worth of testosterone prescriptions. 'I don't know how this will interact with your hormones though,' she said, eventually, softer and more gently now.

I felt relieved. At least I was going to get it.

'I don't know either, but I don't think there's really time to check. My gender clinic doesn't do sexual health, they just do assessments and stuff. There aren't manuals for this. We've just got to figure it out on our own.'

A long pause.

'Right. Well, I can give you this.' She seemed reluctant. 'But on the understanding that you take it at your own risk. I'm not a specialist, so I don't know how it'll affect you.'

'That's fine,' I replied, feeling the blood beginning to drain from my face.

We stood up and went back to the main pharmaceutical counter.

The older guy was *still* looking at plasters. I manoeuvred past him. At least it'd give him a story to tell his wife when he got home.

The pharmacist explained that I should take the pill with water and that sometimes people experience nausea. I didn't really listen. I just wanted her to give it to me and to get out of there. I took the bag, clenched it in my right hand, and left.

Back at home, I poured myself a glass of water from the kitchen tap. I opened the box and saw a pink pill contained in silver foil wrapping and a plastic case that was much too large. *Of course* it would be pink, I thought, rolling my eyes. I took the pill and gulped. Then waited.

I don't know what I expected, really. It's not that I imagined something would happen straight away. But I did feel different somehow. Like the pill was a big decision, even though there was no guarantee of a pregnancy in the first place. It felt significant. And the pharmacist was right; I didn't know what effect what I imagine was a hormone-filled pill would actually have on my body. But what choice did I have?

For the next day or two I did feel strange. I felt sick and quite dizzy, needing to lie down a lot of the time. I started bleeding for the first time in four or five years. I found some sanitary pads in the back of the bathroom cupboard that I'd kept *just in case*. I comforted myself with a hot water bottle and chocolate and by telling myself that this meant it was probably working, but I was still furious that I had to take it in the first place.

Elliot never contacted me again.

The first and only time I accessed non-trans-specific sexual healthcare was an unflinching disaster and, truly, I still feel angry about it. I feel furious that the very place I had gone to receive 'care' turned me away and told me that bodies like mine didn't – couldn't – exist. It doesn't really get more degrading and dehumanizing than that.

The trans healthcare structure as we know it today – accessing gender identity services who assess whether we're trans enough via two psychiatrists – is rooted in a patriarchal field of psychiatry. Doctors throughout the 20th century understood hormone treatment and surgeries as a way of fitting trans people into the rest of society. It was about how well a person could pass. Whether treatment could 'fix' them of their transness. A person could, in their view, move between sexes, just so long as the boundaries and categories of male and female remained intact. Trans healthcare has not historically been about bodily autonomy; it is about fixing people who are seen as broken. So much effort and emphasis has been put on our physical transitions so we fit societal expectations of male and female that the rest of our healthcare, such as sexual health and abortion rights, has been entirely forgotten.

From its inception, trans healthcare has been an ideological battleground. Medical transition, contraception and abortion care *should* be about body autonomy. We should have the right to choose what is the best option for our own bodies and mental health. But instead, when we try to access vital healthcare, we are met by gatekeepers who think they know better than we do about our bodies. Like the pharmacist who stubbornly claimed 'men can't get pregnant' whilst I put myself in a vulnerable position asking for help. Or 'gender specialist' psychiatrists who make assessments that interrogate our gender and try to work out whether we fit into a very narrow framework of what being trans is. While people bicker online and in person about the validity of trans lives, whether we do or don't exist, what bathrooms and spaces we are allowed to access, there are very real, entirely tangible effects on people's actual lives – like me practically begging for protection from an unwanted pregnancy.

Fertility and sexual health is one area of healthcare in which trans people have suffered the greatest medical injustice. Even though the first case of HIV/AIDS was diagnosed in the UK in 1981 and discriminately affected gay men, there is still little to no data on trans and non-binary people living with HIV. In fact, in 2020 I was one of five trans men put on the PrEP (pre-exposure prophylaxis) trial in the UK (PrEP is a drug that stops transmission of HIV). As far as I know, this is the first research to include trans men in HIV care. And in the early 1970s, Sweden became the first country in the world to allow people to change their legal sex. However, they simultaneously implemented compulsory sterilization on the grounds that trans people were mentally ill and therefore unfit to care for kids. Thankfully the UK has never implemented a sterilization policy, but the NHS still refuses to fund trans fertility treatment, such as storing gametes (the freezing of eggs and sperm) before starting hormone treatment. At 18, when I began taking testosterone medication, I had to sign a document to say that I understood that this medication would make me infertile. However, I have since met many trans men who, like I said before, have conceived, even though they took testosterone for several years.

When we talk about trans healthcare, we don't only mean access to hormones and gender-confirming surgeries. That would be like saying that the only healthcare a deaf person accesses is for their hearing. No, trans healthcare is holistic and includes every type of healthcare you can imagine *and* access to gender identity services. This means that every variety of healthcare professional should have basic training in the positive treatment of trans people so that we are not told at the counter that we don't exist or that a GP might not be 'comfortable' with prescribing hormones because they don't have enough knowledge about the topic. Often when I go to the GP about something entirely unrelated, like a chest infection or depression, the conversation always turns back to my transition. Trans broken arm syndrome we call it. Where if we have a broken arm, the professional in some way will try to relate it back to being on hormones, like the hormones are thinning the bones and will make them more likely to break or something. This is nonsense and is grounded in absolutely no research. When I have a regular discussion with my doctor's surgery about the anti-depression medication I am on, they assume that my depression is due to the fact that I am trans, not because of the transphobia and hostility I face, or they fail to consider that maybe I would still have depression even if I were cisgender.

There needs to be an urgent revolution in trans health-care. Not only in flooding money into research and giving all medical staff access to trans-specific training but also in reshaping power and giving body autonomy to all people to decide what is right for them. Trans people are not alone in this struggle. For decades, people living with HIV/AIDS have died from government negligence, stigma in the press, lack of intervention or funding and a belief that they somehow deserve their diagnosis. There has been so much evidence of medical discrimination and abuse in our communities. Our fight for fair, balanced and humane healthcare is a joint one and still continues.

Fuck Me
Then Fuck Off

Honestly, I'd grown tired of all the hook-ups. Of all the messages saying, 'Let's meet soon!!' only to be blocked or ignored after they'd finished their wank. Of opening the front door to a guy who looks nothing like his pictures and the awkward sitting on the bed chatting about their tediously boring sounding job, realizing that I probably didn't want to have sex after all. I just wanted something that felt meaningful and reciprocal.

I'd numbed myself to the point where I no longer wanted real emotional connection or longevity. As the drag saying goes, *fuck me or fuck off*. Cum, then go. And don't cuddle afterwards. I'd made a semi-conscious decision that I didn't want to engage emotionally with anyone any more. I didn't want to hurt again and risk losing another relationship or person I cared so deeply about. And plus, I told myself, this is what your early twenties are for – don't tie yourself down. So I lied to myself and denied myself the love and respect that I craved deep inside while pretending that it was what it meant to be a gay man. To fuck, dance, be the gay best friend, repeat.

I was using sex as a way of confirming what I thought of myself – that sex was all anyone really wanted from me and that it was all I was good for.

Casual sex isn't problematic in terms of morality. I don't, and nor should anyone, judge anyone for their sexual behaviour – how much, how little, when, where, who with – as long as it's all legal and consensual. But using sex to fix emotional problems is something I think we run into a lot as gay men. We try to fix gay shame by having sex, telling ourselves that it's all we really want and all we are really good for, and we reject ourselves in the process. That's what happened to me, anyway.

The second time I went to a gay sauna was very different to the first. I was sober, for a start. I wanted be able to experience it to the full, not weighed down by exhaustion, a hangover come-down or fear of my own body and how others may respond to it. And I was curious what another, more popular sauna with younger men, at a more reasonable hour, would be like.

* * *

I grew nervous as I approached Ramillies Street. I sat on the benches outside, my work backpack hunched on my shoulders, and tried to calm myself down. Is this what I really wanted to do? Why was I so nervous? Would anyone actually be in there at 6 p.m. on a Monday evening? I watched as a bald, trim man entered. He didn't seem to be anxious at all. He walked quickly, head high and confident, utterly non-perturbed by the place he was entering. It may as well have been Boots. I decided to take the opportunity and followed him.

I was surprised to see a queue at the entrance and a video playing above the counter. It was like one of those videos you get at the airport: 'Put your bags and belongings into the cart, sir, and then walk through the metal detector'. The graphic instructional video was explaining how to ask for a key, what belongings to put into the box and what you could have access to once inside. It was satisfying to know that I wasn't the only one who didn't know what the hell I was doing.

Once in and with my locker key strapped to my wrist, I went to the changing area, which was much smaller than the one at the previous sauna. The lockers were more like cages; bags, jeans and socks all stuffed inside, with little protection except for a flimsy plastic padlock. I got undressed, removing my underwear this time, and put the microfibre cloth around my waist before heading downstairs.

The welcome area felt like a leisure centre. You know, the ones with the wave machines that go off every hour and a water slide that's always closed 'for maintenance'. I could smell the stench of chlorine coming from the hot tub, in which sat maybe twenty or so naked men, who all seemed to be chatting jollily enough. In the middle of the room was an array of metal chairs and tables, where empty cans of Fanta and Diet Coke lay abandoned. I sat down at any empty table to get my bearings. One man sat on his phone chatting to someone on Grindr, the familiar orange and blue speech bubbles popping up on his screen. On my right, an older man seemed completely enthralled with *Coronation Street*, which was playing on the television opposite.

I touched my wristband onto the metal turnstile, feeling like either cattle or a football fan, I didn't know which, and made my way, apprehensively, downstairs. The red halogen lighting illuminated my path as I moved deeper underground, and it grew warmer and warmer with each flight. Eventually I reached a black door and slipped inside.

It was steamy. Really steamy. Men showered in the open, moving their hands through their hair and letting the water cascade down their bodies, while others wandered in and out of various doors and hanging plastic dividers. A scald of panic glided through my body. I had no idea what was on the other side but I was intrigued to find out.

I chose the door straight in front of me first. It opened into a room that was intensely hot and empty except for two large men who sat on tiled platforms and weren't speaking to each other. It felt like any other sauna at a leisure centre really. Hot, awkward and silent. Another, younger man followed me in but immediately left when he noticed how quiet it was. I did the same.

The adjacent rooms were real mazes. Small corridors with little light, with more rooms and more shadowy hallways going off in various directions. A real rabbit warren. Each room was concealed enough so it was an effort to enter, needing you to make an effort to look inside, but not so concealed that you felt like you couldn't go in. Some of these entirely tiled rooms had men in them, and others were completely empty. Men would pop their heads in, sit down if they were interested in you and leave if they weren't. As I continued to wander and got deeper into the maze, I could hear mild grunts and slurping. I could hear and smell the sex before I could see it. When I eventually reached the source of the sound, four men were tangled together in a four-way suck off. I could just about make out the shape of their bodies in the glow, their frames outlined by what little light there was. I joined some men on the opposite side of the room who were watching, suddenly very aware of my lack of cock and inability to fully participate. I sat with this for a moment. Acknowledging my empty space. I felt the room grow heavier. The humid air became stickier, denser, hotter.

I got up to leave. Nobody moved. The four strangers continued to twist and writhe into each other. As I walked away, the slurps became more distant, and I was relieved.

Back in the stairwell, I took a breath. It was much colder there, and the drop in temperature was immediately soothing. Despite being in the other room only a matter of moments ago, the door felt like a gateway to another world, one that I wasn't sure was real or not. The blood thumping through my veins started to slow slightly and then, calm.

I spotted stairs downwards I hadn't noticed before. I had assumed that the floor I was on was all there was. I considered if I wanted to go. It took so much courage to be here in the first place, I told myself, you might as well. And you don't *have* to do anything. I felt the emptiness of the floor below calling me, taunting at me to go. So I did.

Downstairs was even darker than upstairs. There wasn't one continuous source of light. It flashed red then green, then white. Like the shittiest club you've ever been in. The rooms here were split into cubicles. Sort of like the unisex changing rooms you get at swimming pools. Doors with terrible plastic locks with space at both the top and the bottom. Most of the doors to these small cubicles were shut.

I made my way round, past a cage with a leather sling in it, past two guys who were tossing each other off and another just sitting waiting, as if the N18 bus was going to come any time.

I heard a noise. A rustling. I followed, my curiosity getting the better of me. In the corner, behind the cage with the sling, was a tiny alcove, in which six, maybe seven, guys stood.

More than I'd seen in the rest of the room combined. Some wore towels, some did not, and they fucked, their breathy moans fuelling one another and egging each other on. I stood, not really knowing what to do next.

Then a hand, a fumbling in the dark, searching for me. A bodiless arm reached for my groin in a cup, looking for what was not there. He grabbed at it again, convinced he'd find what he wanted. I knew he wouldn't. He pushed me face-first against the wall, and I could almost taste the brickwork. There was a black plastic pipe tied to the wall next to me. I hadn't noticed it before. I wondered if they were for water or sewage. We were the rats underground, squirrelling around in a dark maze. The hand reached from behind me into the pipe and grabbed two condoms and lube.

'Follow me,' he said.

I don't know why I followed. I don't know if I wanted to or not. I don't know if that matters.

In one of the cubicles he de-robed me. I lay on my back with nothing but a blue plastic mat underneath me for support. It reminded me of one of those mats you get when you're learning gymnastics in the school hall.

I didn't see his face, but I sensed his shock. He put his hand to my pussy, as if asking where my penis was. It's the same question I asked myself sometimes too. His surprise, my reveal, doesn't cause his hard-on to falter. He lubes up and slides into me. And I say nothing.

Red
White
Green
Red
White

Green
Red
  White
    Green

The lights flash to the rhythm of his thrusts.

I become aware of the mechanics of my own body, noticing the things that would usually go unnoticed.

He spits on his hand, smearing it on me. Whether for his enjoyment or mine, it's hard to tell.

Then he asks, 'Do you bleed?'

'*What?*' A beat.

'Am I bleeding?'

'No.'

'Do you bleed...from here?' He points at my pussy.

I sit up, removing him from me. '*What? I don't know what you're asking.*' I know full well what he's asking.

'Just lie back down.'

'*No I think I've had enough.*'

'But I'm not finished.'

I find my words and my strength. '*I am.*'

I pick up my towel and notice used condoms lying next to me. The remainder of what went before. I wonder how many guys he'd taken here before me.

I move to the changing room quickly, checking intermittently that he's not following.

Stepping back into my black skinny jeans, I feel nothing at all, really. It's kind of a blur. I don't feel like my feet are on the ground. I feel like I'm somewhere else – floating in and out of gender, maybe. I don't feel scared, or foolish, or happy, or relieved, or sad. But I do think I feel strong. Strong enough to be here. Strong enough to leave. Strong enough to remove my body from the violence I had subjected myself to. Strangely, I left feeling like I loved myself more.

* * *

I relayed this story to someone once. They asked me if I regretted going to the sauna. Whether I thought it was non-consensual or sexual violence or something. I said I didn't think it was. I'd chosen to go with him after all, and besides, that wasn't really the point. I didn't regret going to the sauna because it unveiled something within me that I needed to acknowledge. Maybe I needed to go to an extreme in order to hear it. And listen.

It's important to say that not all sauna, fetish or cruising nights are like this. In fact, when in the right headspace, looking out for yourself and your own personal safety, these places can be enjoyable, places to experience new things and sexual liberation. People go for the otherworldliness, for intrigue, for anonymity, for pleasure; and they find it. I have found it too. But I have also learned to take care of myself better, to not follow blindly and walk towards violence. My trips to these kinds of spaces now involve going with friends, setting boundaries, telling people where I am and not feeling pressure to have sex just because I'm in a place surrounded by it. But most of all, I have learned that cruising in saunas and having sex with men makes me no more a man, or no more gay, than if I didn't. These, I realized, are not the things that define us.

Lockdown

The 2020 Covid-19 lockdown was a right pain in the arse for everyone. We all imprisoned ourselves for the benefit of each other, and with that went seeing family, friends and lovers; dates; jobs; hobbies; trips to the cinema; getting on busses...life as we knew it. And we had no idea when we'd be able to do any of those things again.

I'd never felt trapped in London before. London was, for me, a place of possibility. In such a large city with diversity of people, arts, museums and libraries and endless events, I had always felt like I could go anywhere, really. But now I had nothing but my four walls for company. For me, that was terrifying.

It was around this time I started seeing a therapist to help me look at the walls without panicking. To slow down. I knew I was filling every inch of my diary to be busy enough to avoid those niggling thoughts at the back of my head. Horrible thoughts about never being able to find someone to love again or whether I'd ever fit in the gay community as a gay trans man. I remember being terrified when the lockdown was announced because it meant I'd be alone. No more late-night hook-ups when I couldn't get to sleep or filling my diary with activities so I didn't have to sit around long enough to look at myself. When the lockdown first hit, I realized I hadn't actually been home for a single evening in eight weeks. I was exhausted.

Therapy, for me, didn't so much focus on changing everyday behaviours; it was more about looking to my past and how that might inform my current and future decisions. We broke everything down, from my childhood and growing up in gendered spaces, puberty and fierce gender expectations. We discussed confusion about my sexuality which felt like a pendulum, the loss of a long-term relationship and how I'd turned to inflicting violence on myself as a way of coping. Violence was what felt familiar, offering the tightest of hugs. But I didn't want to hurt any more. Not really. I wanted to end the cycle of being cruel to myself. And for that, I needed to rethink, relearn and take notice of myself more. If I wanted to be happy without the constant need for *more* boys, *more* sex, *more* affirmation, then I needed to realize that partying wasn't a journey towards myself. It was running away.

I knew that at home, with nothing else to do than stay put, was the best opportunity for me to rethink and give myself the best chance to succeed. This meant *not* cutting dates off too early because I assumed they would end badly. It also meant letting someone care for me if they wanted to, rather than putting up my guard and assuming they would leave – because in my mind, everyone did in the end. It meant allowing myself to see my trans body as just that – a trans body – not something to compare to cis bodies. It meant seeing my body and beauty in its own right and believing that others might be able to see that too. And finally, it meant forgiveness and understanding that not everyone will 'get it', and that is okay.

Covid-19 abruptly stopped my rejection cycle. It wasn't welcome. I wanted to fuck and dance and hurt. But a state-enforced lockdown put an end to my man-to-man-to-man-to-man behaviour. The eight or nine guys I'd been chatting to fell away one by one when we realized we wouldn't be able to meet up and the lockdown was going to last more than a few weeks. The virtual dates, watching a movie and ordering a Chinese at the same time, and sending the same nudes over and over wasn't really going to cut it. So slowly the boys peeled away and I was left with only myself.

I don't think I'm alone in feeling like lockdown forced me to really think about what I wanted and where I was going. Was I happy in my job and was I going to change it? Was I ready for a relationship and, if so, what might that person's personality be like? Was my forever home in London? What were my future and possibilities?

I've never been good at looking to the future. I'm okay with a near future – two or three years, say – but anything beyond that feels too big. Too vast. It's difficult to see or plan for a long future when you couldn't see any future for yourself when growing up. I couldn't see anyone who looked or felt like me, so in some ways I didn't know a future was possible. I wrote in my introduction that as a child I could never see a future past 'male'. I still can't really. So these were huge, overwhelming questions that I'd never given myself the opportunity to think properly about before.

I worked with my therapist to figure out a plan. We imagined what life could look like. We imagined possibilities. Were those possibilities of having children, or of having gender-affirming surgery, or having a husband, or obtaining a gender recognition certificate to be recognized as male under the law? Or maybe life would bring none of those things. Perhaps it was about finding ease in my own body. To worry less about 'fitting in' and finding my own place and being at peace with my differences. Success for me didn't necessarily have to be about a job, or boyfriend, or new flat, or car. Success could just as much be about enjoying a swim and not being so conscious of my hips or scars. Success could look like allowing someone to love me and stopping rejecting myself. It was liberating to feel like anything was possible and to finally, after twenty-odd years, see a future that was in reach.

I talked to my therapist a lot about boys. Boys who had gone by, boys who I was currently seeing, boys who I wished I was seeing... Although I'd gone on dates, had sex with cis gay men, I hadn't yet managed to find a boyfriend, despite wanting to. I suppose what was scarier than going into gay bars, cruising spaces and saunas was making myself open to love and trusting someone again. That's hard following any long-term relationship that has been broken down and being subject to so much rejection, violence and erasure from all parts of our society. It took a long time to decipher what my fears were about getting into a relationship again. I thought I was ready, but I had no idea where to start.

Fear #1

I noticed that many men in the gay community have a forever young mentality – Peter Pan syndrome, we sometimes call it. When people say, 'They've been together six months, which is almost three decades in gay years', what they mean to say is that gay men have a reputation of being sexually promiscuous and moving on quickly. I don't think there is any shame in doing that; after all, life is for enjoying, and there are no rules to say that we should only be with one person forever. One of the best things about queerness is stepping away from heteronormative standards and enjoying all kinds of relationships, whether monogamous or polyamorous or just hook-ups. The majority of queer people don't have to hold down long-term relationships for the sake of family approval or children, especially when it's not working. From what I can see, I think gay men are getting more comfortable with ageing and have older couples to look up to. In short, we can see what our futures as gay men might look like.

For a long time, we didn't have a blueprint of what older relationships could be. This was, in part, due to the illegality of homosexuality, gay shame, a requirement to hide in the shadows and the AIDS crisis of the late eighties onwards. Huge numbers of young gay men died way before their time. In their prime, really. We have lost hundreds of thousands of gay men, who, if still around now, would comfortably be in their sixties and seventies. They should be here. For a long time, gay and trans people didn't have a map or pathway to follow. We couldn't see what growing older queer might look like – what our possibilities were. What our weddings might look like (gay marriage was only legalized in the UK in 2014), what possibilities there might be for children or what our lives could look like without children. In a sense, we're still in the infancy of living out our lives in their entirety without the need to hide. We're still making it up as we go along. For some that's a really exciting prospect: doing things on our own terms. For others it's daunting.

There's a lot of trauma – both personal and generational – in the gay community. It's not surprising that many people want to have as much fun as possible and not get 'tied down'. So much of our heritage has been about having fun while it lasts, because you never know which night out might be your last. Understanding the heavy weight of this, I wondered whether I might find another gay man who wanted a long-term relationship. I knew gay men who had successful relationships for a long time, but most of the people I had contact with wanted something casual. So I was worried about trying. Putting myself out there and falling hard (classic Harry), looking for something long term only to be rejected, understandably, by men looking for something casual.

Fear #2

My fear about dating men and that potentially turning into a relationship was also in part about allowing myself to be vulnerable. It's fairly easy for me now to have sex with someone without knowing their name, but it is much harder to make a real connection, and I fear being rejected and hurt somewhere along the way. At least with casual sex, it's in and out (pun intended) with no expectation of emotional responsibility or support. But I knew, deep down, that I was denying myself a chance at happiness. Relationships aren't for everyone, but they are for me. I knew I had to try.

Fear #3

Another fear when contemplating a relationship with a mystery man was how they might respond to my transness. Many of my trans friends talk of only being T4T – trans for trans – only having sex and dating other trans people because they 'get it'. I understand this on some level. It's comforting to know that the person you're with understands, to some degree, what you're going through. But I didn't want to restrict myself in this way. Not only because the pool of trans people is relatively small but also because not all trans people are the same. We may not experience dysphoria in the same way (or at all), experience family rejection or have hang-ups about our bodies. And in any case, most people in my life are cisgender. Although these people can sometimes ask strange, difficult questions, they almost always come from a place of wanting to support and understand. I suppose I didn't care as much about them 'getting it'. I was concentrating more on them 'getting me'.

Fear #4

Being in a relationship is never just about that one person who you're in a relationship with. It's also about their family and their friends. So although he might be the loveliest, sexiest, horniest, most accepting, thoughtful dream of a man, I worried if me being trans might be a red flag for his family. Good enough in the sheets but not good enough for Sunday lunch with their parents – that kind of thing. These fears came from the notion that trans people are inherently unlovable. That we have complex, trauma-filled histories and therefore we're complicated and it all might get a bit tricky. And because transness doesn't always show itself, that might mean another (!) nerve-wracking coming out for me, where my own feelings and future are at stake.

I had a lot of time during lockdown to think about these fears and attempt to tackle them head on. I might not have been dating or having sex at the time, but that gave me the perfect opportunity to reflect, grow and assess what I wanted once we were allowed to leave our houses and socialize again.

A lot of strength came from discussing each of these fears at length, tackling and questioning them head on, thinking about what their roots were and how they might show up in my life. It was tricky and difficult to interact with these questions. I had to notice how much of this way of thinking was my own fears projected onto others and I had to allow myself the opportunity of love – even if some of my fears did reveal themselves in the process. And if they did, how might I react in a self-respecting way? This was a whole new idea to me. I'd never approached anything in my life in an intentionally 'self-respecting way'. I'd approached everything in a let's-fuck-and-get-drunk kind of way. But apparently, that's not what a therapist suggests. So when I started to message a handsome Scottish boy living in East London with thick, dark hair and eyes to die for, I knew it was time to put these new therapeutic lessons into practice.

Nightcall(s)

'd had my eye on Liam for a while. In the November before the first lockdown, we had matched on Chappy – a dating app for gay men that sadly no longer exists. It was a bit like Hinge, but without all the annoying questions. We messaged back and forth into the early hours, as you do in those first days. Eventually we followed each other on Twitter, the benefit of which being that I could stalk back on his photos that he'd posted over the last few months. After a few days of intense discussion about beige buffets, the social media hellscape and diabolical political escapades, the conversation fizzled out. I don't think it was because we weren't interested in each other. It wasn't even because the conversation went dry. It was just that life got busy – he was working on an event for World AIDS Day and looking for a new flat, and I was planning for Christmas and had multiple boys to respond to – exhausting.

It wasn't until way after the lockdown had started (and I'd had a hell of a lot of therapy) that we picked up messaging again. Around the same time, I had decided that it would be a good idea to try to get into running. I like to pretend that this had something to do with looking after my physical health, given that we legally only had one hour to leave the house a day, but it absolutely wasn't. Liam is a fantastic long-distance runner, and I wanted to find an excuse to talk to him, so I asked questions like 'What technique is best?' and 'What shoes should I buy?' A bit lame, but what else is there to ask?

It turned out that running was a terrible idea. I lost my breath, tore my calf muscle and generally loathed the whole thing, but I'd caught Liam at a good moment. As it turned out, he'd been thinking about his life, previous and potential relationships and the direction of travel for his career too. He'd just been let down by a boy he was really into. The boy he fancied had asked Liam to come over to his, which Liam did, only to tell him moments later that he was going on a date with someone else...shit or what? He was keeping Liam as a reserve and Liam, after months of this, had enough. So it was fortuitous, he said, that we'd decided to start messaging again.

With little to distract us, we spent our evenings in our respective flats on opposite ends of the Central line, looking out of our windows, feeling the breeze and longing for each other. Weeks, months, passed by and we hadn't been able to see each other in person, despite texting all day and FaceTiming each night. It was only an hour Tube ride, we were in the same city, and yet he could have been anywhere in the world. He felt so far away. Each night we decided on an album to listen to together. His dad had introduced him to music – 'all the good shit' – and I wanted to learn. We messaged throughout, giving our thoughts and what we liked. 'Come Together' by Primal Scream and 'Nightcall' by London Grammar became our songs and my most-listened-to tunes that year.

We couldn't meet each other because the world was shut, so voice notes became our primary method of communication. They felt like contemporary love letters, and I wondered whether this was how it used to be. Before Grindr and hook-ups and dating apps. I was used to fucking first, friends later, so this felt novel. We were getting to know each other first. It was refreshing. It felt new. It felt good. We just had to hope that the same connection would carry through when – if – we could ever meet in person.

We played tennis on our first date. Conveniently for me it's my favourite sport – handy because it was pretty much the only sport we could do at distance, given the rules about no people from separate households being in close contact. I brought my tennis racquet, a spare, and tennis balls. He brought a fruit picnic – complete with strawberries. We may as well have just eaten the picnic, because Liam was terrible at tennis. Like, *really* bad. As in, he hit the tennis ball over the fence and it landed straight into someone's barbecue, right on top of the sausages. We had to evacuate because the smoke filled the tennis court.

Now a whole tube of tennis balls down, we had to think of what our next date would be when restrictions eased a little. Liam, being a much better runner than I could ever be, challenged himself to run from his flat in Mile End, East London, to mine in West London. It was 12.9 miles. Just under a half marathon. I thought it sounded like hell, but he said he missed the feeling of a race day and was up for the challenge – all I had to do was provide him with a glass of water and a kiss when he finished. And that's a challenge I was up for. Feeling suitably inadequate by not running 12.9 miles and utterly besotted with him, I wanted to do something. So with a cardboard box from a neighbour's Amazon delivery and some tin foil I found in the cupboard, I made a running bib with his name and the date on, along with a tin-foil medal with a smiley face and 'congratulations – nearly a half marathon' written in black Sharpie. As Liam ran up the street, I pulled up the window and cheered him on, much to the disdain of my neighbours, but I didn't care. I was just so happy to see him.

When he reached me, Liam ran straight into my arms and kissed me for the first time. It was a surprisingly gentle kiss for someone who had run for two hours across London. His lips were knowing and considerate. His body folded into mine as I put the white string that I had used to make the tinfoil medal over his head and I could feel the sweat weeping from his body. I didn't mind. I just felt happy that he'd finished his run and that he'd chosen me to run to. We spent the rest of the afternoon in my flat's communal garden listening to nineties music shimmying from speakers. Bliss.

* * *

The 27th June of 2020 was meant to be the start of London Pride and Glastonbury weekend. Predictably, neither Pride nor Glastonbury went ahead. With very few actual events taking place, Liam and I decided to mark the occasions ourselves. Queer people have always had a 'let's rally and do it ourselves' attitude, so it felt entirely natural.

We found the planned Pride route online and followed it using Citymapper. We walked hand in hand through the emptier-than-usual streets of London, reminiscing about Prides gone by. Prides with exes, Liam marching with the Terrence Higgins Trust and I with Stonewall. We've both marched at London Pride, Manchester Pride and Student

Pride before, and at the same time, but we weren't aware of each other then. We circled the same spaces but had never met. It was comforting to share the memories together and build our own, private, first Pride. As we neared the end of the route, approaching The Mall, we kissed. It felt just as powerful and symbolic to do it alone as it would have done if there were crowds there. We don't take public affection for granted. It's not something that's always been given to us as gay people, and it always carries a safety risk. Acknowledging this to each other, it made it feel even more momentous. We vowed to kiss again in the same spot when the world reopened and London Pride went ahead.

Even though Glastonbury didn't take place, it was decided by the BBC that putting previous years' sets online to watch on iPlayer would boost national morale and unite through the power of music. They were right. Liam and I watched, popcorn in hand, wrapped in each other's bodies, sharing the summer heat. Midway through David Bowie's set, I whispered in Liam's ear that I loved him. He paused before saying that he loved me too.

That night, we stayed up late and listened to disco music on speakers. We danced together, practising for when the gay bars would eventually reopen. They were silly dances, terrible hip jives and flailing arms. We imagined the disco balls above. The sticky floors. The pulsating lights. It was the freest I'd felt in months.

I'd almost forgotten that we were in a gay relationship during lockdown. We both love being gay – it's central to who we are – but our difference doesn't define us. In fact, we're not 'different' when we're together. Were both gay, so we don't feel alienated by our queerness in the same way we would when out in the 'real world'. We were just Liam and Harry. We were people first, categories second. We exist outside of semantics and boxes. Lockdown was good like that. We could exist in our own little bubbles and worlds, free from any judgement or harassment.

Unfortunately when back in the outside world, this freedom didn't last long. Liam and I walked side by side looking vaguely gay. And by that I mean fitted T-shirts, shorts that were shorter than the ones they sell in Debenhams and those socks with the two stripes on. A classic gay boy look for reasons I don't understand. It's just sort of an unspoken agreement. There was a group of boys on bikes doing that annoying wheely thing they do: putting their front wheel high in the air and riding on their back wheel. They must think they look cool or that it makes them look like they've got big dicks or something, but really they just look like twats. And yes, I'm saying that because I do feel intimidated whenever I see it. One lad shouted 'Gay boys!' at us as they cycled past. Then the others followed. An echo of 'Gay boys, gay boys, gay boys.' Having not come into contact with anything like this for some time, Liam was shaken and upset. It wasn't a particularly vicious event, nor was the sentiment of their chant untrue, but understandably he didn't like being shouted at. Being shouted homophobic abuse, especially something as simple as 'gay boy' is strange. I can only assume that it's to embarrass and 'reveal' us somehow. For a long time, gay men tried to hide their gayness (with difficulty), and so a reveal was a real threat. Nowadays, many gay men don't feel the need to hide it as much, so I found it an interesting hangover from more homophobic times. That and clearly they couldn't think of anything more creative to say.

I thought I should be more upset by the shouting than I was. Of course I was bothered by it and I feel sadness when

Liam does – I want to make things better and protect him in some way – but I wasn't so bothered by it myself. If anything, it was also nice to be acknowledged. For a complete stranger to see me as a gay boy and us as a gay couple. It was almost like a confirmation – a rite of passage – for a label I'd worked so hard for.

* * *

One late summer evening, Liam and I wandered the city. It was dark and quiet with pub curfews still being at 10 p.m. We just wanted a walk next to the Thames, to feel less cooped up and remember we were still in London, not just in some boxy flat that could be in the middle of nowhere.

That night, I decided I wanted to be honest. I knew Liam was a careful boy, never wanting to upset anyone, and he is very considerate about everything he says. But I wanted to dig deeper, know a little more about how he was feeling about himself, me and what our relationship was starting to become. I didn't want him to feel like he had to carry it all on his own or protect me by not talking about things that affected us both. I knew there is much toxicity and so many mistruths peddled around transness and gay relationships, so I wanted to be able to discuss them openly, and together.

I asked if Liam had any anxiety about dating a trans man. It was a big question, and understandably Liam was tentative about replying. I encouraged him by saying that he could say anything and it wouldn't change how I felt about him or the relationship we had. Liam said that his anxiety around dating a gay trans man mainly came from not having the knowledge about how to properly support someone who is trans. Although he'd worked with a few older trans people at the Terrence Higgins Trust, working on inclusive sexual health campaigns and advocacy work, lobbying for PrEP and reporting for trans people, that was more of a professional relationship. He had knowledge of transness in a very direct, literal way (related to bodies and sexual health) but hadn't had the experience with a close friend or partner before, so the emotional support required and the understanding of how the media onslaught affected an individual was new. He was all too aware of the hostile discourse from the press, the same as I was. He said, 'Selfishly, I am worried I won't be able to give you the support you deserve when these things come up.' He was fearful of others, especially gender critical ideologists, and didn't want to let them or their views affect me or undermine the relationship we had.

I think this is a common feeling for trans allies, close friends and partners. They see and witness so much hurt and are not directly targeted, but it still affects them. They can see how much it pains us and know that they can't take that away, so they feel helpless. I told Liam that the best thing he could do was listen, which was exactly what he was doing already.

When we were eventually able, and not under some government-enforced sex ban, Liam came over to mine. We'd already discussed at length, over the several months we'd been talking via voice notes, what we were into, what kind of sex we enjoyed, what we'd experienced so far and what we might want our sex to look like. It was all very healthy, really, which was not something I was used to. So when the time came, I felt excited, at ease and nervous in equal measure for the experience to live up to what I hoped.

Sometimes the world can be a cruel mistress. And she really bloody was that day, because the afternoon that Liam was coming over I came on my period. Being six, nearly seven, years on testosterone, I don't bleed much, or at all really. It was entirely out of the blue. My testosterone levels must have been low or something. I phoned Liam.

'Hey, I'm really sorry but I've...uh...it's a bit difficult. I've come on my period.'

'Oh. That's okay, don't worry! Do you still want me to come over or do you want some space?'

'Oh, right. Erm, no I'd still like you to come over...but only if you want to!'

'Yeah, I really do! I just meant if you weren't feeling up to it. I can bring snacks and cuddles.'

Liam grew up in a matriarchal household with two powerhouse sisters, a proud mother and a supportive father, so the idea of supporting people through periods and the menopause came very naturally to him. I needn't have worried. Liam knew exactly what to do, offering support, space and hot water bottles whenever I needed.

The period ended up being some kind of short freak shower, and we did end up having sex that night. Weirdly the bleeding and cramps just stopped, so I jumped at the opportunity. Maybe it was stress. As I expected, the sex was thoughtful, sensual and incredibly caring: everything I hoped it would be.

Afterwards we lay in each other's arms embracing each other. I don't know if it was the post-cum bliss or the vulnerability of the day that made me ask, or maybe it was just the fact I like to indulge in post-sex analysis, but I wanted to know how it was for him and if it had matched up to his expectations of what he thought it would be like, knowing that he hadn't had sex with a trans guy before. Liam said that while single and having sex with cis men, his primary concern had been avoid avoiding HIV infection through safer sex – PrEP and condoms – but having sex with me meant the risk had reduced (not entirely, but by a substantial amount in statistical terms) and now the need was for protection against pregnancy. I asked if that concerned him. To my relief, he said no. He knew I was on the pill and trusted me to take it, and we used condoms. We were safe, and if anything did happen, he said he would support me through it. Nothing, and I mean nothing, is any better than hearing that kind of support and reassurance. Men have a bad reputation for running when things get tough or for being thoughtless about the impacts of sex for people who have vaginas. I don't know whether it was Liam's background in sexual health, his natural ability to be understanding and put me at ease or both, but I fell in love with him even more that day.

Because I'm naturally nosey and he brought up pregnancy first, I asked Liam if he wanted or had ever thought about having kids. Understandably, his eyes widened and he looked frightened before I reassured him that it was all hypothetical chat. I did not want children any time soon, if at all. He reflected and said that, having had relationships and sex with gay cis men, it hadn't really been on his radar. Of course, same-sex couples could have children through interventions such as IVF, adoption and surrogacy, but this was something slightly different. Here was the potential of having a biological child in the future, both of ours, while being two gay men. A new possibility he hadn't really considered had opened to him, which was a potentially exciting and inviting prospect.

Queerness in all its forms does open up possibility. To be queer is to reject boundaries that have been imposed upon us – what clothes we should wear, who we can fall in love with, who we have sex with and what our bodies can look like, what our futures can be. What Liam was describing was new possibilities of being. Of embracing ourselves and our bodies at the same time as respecting our identities as gay men.

Since then, Liam and I have had a lot of sex – shocker – and it feels as though each time it gets better and better. Not that it was bad to start with (far from it), and I've had *a lot* of bad sex, so I should know. The sex we have is fun, sometimes experimental, but mostly filled with love. When I asked Liam what he likes about the sex we have he said, 'It feels so good,' which is a nice confidence boost for me. In comparison to other relationships he's had in the past, we have more sex than he had with exes. I found this surprising. Why would we be having more sex? Is that just because my sex drive is higher or because we're still in a honeymoon phase or something?

Then Liam said something I hadn't thought of. In past relationships with cis men, having penetrative sex would mean a hell of a lot of prep work. Douching is invasive, takes a long time and has a narrow time frame for when people can have sex. Then, when having sex, dependent on how experienced the person bottoming was, the top might not be able to go particularly fast or for a long period of time before it is too uncomfortable. So much so that in long-term relationships, where the initial flare and passion has now subsided somewhat, douching to facilitate anal sex can feel invasive and quite a lot of work. Around 30 minutes of prep work for a few moments of fun, so other methods of intimacy (like oral sex) become more primary. In the sex that we were having, however, Liam liked that we had options for the type of sex we had. We could have vaginal sex and it could be spontaneous because it doesn't involve as much prep work, or we could have anal sex if that's what we were both wanting. Sex with me, he said, offered more opportunities for pleasure and intimacy with each other.

Then I asked him the question that had been on my mind since we started dating. The question that burns through my mind every time I have sex with a cis man. 'Do you miss dick?' Essentially, did he feel, like I do, like there is a penis missing? He replied, 'No. You're not missing anything. I love your vagina and I would love your penis equally if you chose to have one. Our sex is no less or no more gay, whatever you have. Reducing gayness down to only body parts means ignoring all the other amazing parts of ourselves and our community – being seen as a gay couple in society, clothing, our clubs and bars, our gay history, our Pride. You are so much more than your body...and I love your body. I'll keep telling you that until you believe it.' Then I gave him the longest, happiest kiss I have ever given anyone, and after that I started to believe him.

This was a huge sea change from what I thought – feared – being a gay trans man would be like. At best, I thought it might mean a relationship without having vaginal sex or without talking so openly about bodies. At worst, it meant being alone forever. But that wasn't the case. Here was a man not only willing to accept me as I am but encouraging me to be open and honest, allowing me to explore and experience pleasure in my own way. He was actively helping me to find comfort in my own skin, rather than changing or adapting myself to fit limiting ideas of what it is to be a gay man and what that label can mean.

Words and labels are incredibly important – I love being

gay and trans and wearing those labels with pride – but they should breathe life into us rather than suck it out. We should let the light in rather than close a door on it, expanding our horizon of gayness and transness to mean whatever the hell we want them to mean. They're ours to own. Expanding the landscape of labels means removing the enforcement and policing of the gender we are assigned at birth and what we *should* be like. It makes room for us to decide how we want to live out our lives and what freedom looks like for us. We can grow into ourselves rather than someone else's idea of us. For me, that's the epitome of LGBTQ+ pride and why the LGB and the T can never be torn apart. It's the same fight. It's about rejecting the prison of sexuality and gender that was inflicted on us without our consent and saying, 'No, that does not fit me.' This fight is about freedom, escaping the barriers and systems that force us all down, and battling to live authentically away from binary, heteronormative struc- tures. It's about being outsiders and owning it. It's about rejecting those who seek to control our authentic lives and dampen us down. Queerness is about creating a new space for us *all*.

Liam and I have been together for over two years now. Most of that has been in some kind of lockdown or other. There are things couples do on their first dates, like going to the cinema, that we're still yet to tick off our list. We've kind of done everything backwards. Moving in first and only now starting to do those datey things like going to restaurants and the theatre, meeting friends and planning holidays.

We moved in together properly in June 2021. We found a

flat in West London we both liked and decided it was time to make a home. After years of sharing fridges with flatmates and being evicted from dodgy London sublets, we wanted some stability. A base where we could return to each other. We knew it was risky – relatively, we hadn't known each other that long – but if lockdown taught us anything, it is that nothing is ever guaranteed.

When Liam and I moved in, it was important to both of us that the home we created was queer. So much of trans and gay existence is about space – how much space are we allowed to take up, which spaces we feel safe in, what spaces are designed with us in mind. I don't mean queering space just in queer artwork on the walls or having a Progress Pride flag in the window (although, yes, please!), I mean queering space as in not shying away from having gay books on display, having vials of testosterone in the bathroom, wearing jock-straps around the house, having poppers in the top drawer, mixing our socks and underwear drawers, having photos of us smiling and laughing with each other's families. Queering our home is about not censoring ourselves.

When I thought about this, I felt sad for the gay couples in the past who weren't able to do this so openly and freely. I thought of the boyfriends who would have to rush to their partner's houses when they died before the family got there to remove photos and anything that might out them. I was reminded of this because I read a *BBC News* article with the headline 'Duncan Grant: Artist's "lost" erotic drawing worth £2m discovered'[1] on the same day we were looking

1   Jones, R. (2020) 'Duncan Grant: Artist's "Lost" Erotic Drawings Worth £2m Discovered.' *BBC News*, 8 October, 2020. Accessed on 25/08/2022 at www.bbc.co.uk/news/entertainment-arts-54447684

for flats. Duncan's drawings of gay men in the midst of intimacy had been passed from lover to lover, friend to friend, in secret, because at the time he lived, homosexuality was still illegal. Then one day the artworks were simply...handed in. Unfortunately, this is the fate of a lot of queer history. Relatives and partners destroyed a lot of queer history to protect the reputation of the person who had died or the reputation of their family. And so it is important to both me and Liam, as proud gay men and queer history enthusiasts, to honour gay men who have come before us by living our lives and queering our space as I imagine they would have liked to.

On our way to moving in, a new account followed me on Twitter. They were called Proud Cleaning. I was intrigued, so I messaged them. Were they just really proud of their cleaning techniques or was it something queer related? The owner, Martin, got back in touch and said he'd been anxious about allowing cleaners into his home. He said he'd had cleaners refuse to clean the flat he lives in with his husband on the basis that there was only one bedroom and two men living there. He said that he'd felt the need to pre-clean and hide away any hint of gayness in his home in fear that items would be broken or something. He said that cleaning is intensely personal – you find out all sorts about people. What they're interested in by their books, games, music. What kind of medication they're on by the packets of tablets left in the bathroom. Who their friends are by the photos in frames and pinned to the fridge door. What kind of sex you're into if drawers are left open with sex toys housed inside. He didn't want to hide himself any more, and being laid off during the pandemic had given him an opportunity to address it. I thought it was a brilliant, innovative idea, so I invited them round and I've supported their business ever since.

* * *

The relationship I have with Liam is different to the one I had with Lucy, and not just because they're different people. After Lucy and I broke up, I wondered how I'd ever be able to love anyone again. It turns out I could, I just needed to learn a lot and accept parts of myself I'd avoided first.

My relationship with Liam is often about the mundane, domestic things – the everyday boring shit people in all relationships have to think about – rather than existential questions about the inner workings of sexuality and gender and why things don't fit. The love Liam and I share is much more about if we're having noodles or rice for tea, and if he's remembered to put the white washing on, more than it's about what makes and doesn't make a gay man. It's much easier and more comfortable to be in a relationship when you've figured out the important stuff, rather than trying to battle against normative ideas of gender and sexuality, which only force us down.

I used to think that a gay relationship was unattainable for me. I thought I'd have to grow old alone and adopt too many cats. Then I found out I am allergic to cats, which ruined that idea. Really, I worried that I didn't care enough for myself and therefore I wouldn't be able to care for anyone else. I worried that not having a penis would be an issue for some gay men and it would limit the sex, and therefore relationships, I would be able to have. And maybe it does for some. That's where some gay men draw the line, but that's okay because other men don't. Once, I worried that being gay and trans meant being unlovable. Now I can see how wrong I was.

I'm in a strong and better place now. I'm confident and happy in where I am, but it's taken a lot of learning and work.

It's meant going back and examining pain and where it comes from. Some of that pain is from things a lot of trans and gay people experience – rejection, misunderstanding, bullying and discrimination. Even as the discrimination against trans people from LGB people rises and the transphobia in the UK reaches unbearable, relentless hostility from the British press and this government, I feel hopeful about the future. Trans and gay people share far more similarities than we do differences. And ultimately, that is what ties us together. That's why it will *always* be LGBTQ+. United together. I hope and believe that for future generations of gay and trans people, it won't be such an uphill, exhausting struggle.

I have reached a point in my life where I am not concerned with trying to pass as anything. I'm not interested in looking male, or looking gay, or looking anything, really. I can't pretend to be anything other than the person I am. I'm clumsy like that. I can only do me.

I've been thinking about where my new-found strength and power comes from. I have no doubt that some of it is from being inspired by all the incredible trans performers and authors who have written with far more knowledge and flair than I have about what it is to exist. Before that, I didn't know if there was anyone else like me out there. I'm talking specifically here about the work of Travis Alabanza and Juno Roche, who, if you haven't read already, I wholeheartedly recommend. My power now comes from unity and a knowledge that LGBTQ+ people are resilient. It comes from the amazing trans people I know and see who I could have only dreamt of growing up. It comes from my incredible partner and best friend, who I hope to spend the rest of my life with. It comes from my supportive family – both biological and chosen – who offer me so much love. It comes from the diverse lives we lead that offer endless possibilities of what it means to be a gay and trans person. I'm starting to see the shift. I'm beginning to see more people coming out and being open about who they are. Chiyo, a gay trans man, being named Mr Gay England and being on the front of *Attitude* magazine in 2020 felt like a huge step forward for gay and trans unity. I know there are more of us out there. I'm seeing gay and trans people more and more at Prides and online, and it feels like we're entering into a new space and understanding. I can't wait to meet more of you.

Afterword

At the point of publication, I'll be 26. During my relatively short lifetime, I have lived as a girl, a questioning person, a man, straight, lesbian and gay. I've been all of LGBTQ+ and I'm so proud of that. I've slipped through more identities on the path to finding my 'true' self and learned more perspectives than most people are able to in a lifetime. I think that's a kind of superpower. To have (literally) been in multiple pairs of shoes and seen what life is like from different perspectives. I, and so many of the trans men I know, fight to detoxify masculinity and bring a contemporary version of masculinity, which invests in nuances and understanding. A masculinity that supports women, is rooted in feminist views and comes from a place of understanding of the patriarchy in its various forms. A masculinity with lived experience of girlhood.

Some trans people don't want to acknowledge the gender they were assigned at birth. They say they've always been male/female/non-binary but the world labelled them wrong. I get that. That's valid. I kind of feel that too. If anyone asked me, 'How long have you felt like a boy?' I'd say forever. But at the same time, I want to acknowledge the person who believed at one point they maybe were a girl or a lesbian, or questioning. The journey. The identities that allowed me to rest where I am today, I think, are important. They're still part of me. They aren't to be buried or mourned or forgotten. They live within me, and inform every decision I make and every moment I am in. I try to use those experiences for good.

Despite the myriad of questioning and genders and sexualities I have explored, I am young. I know I haven't got all of this right. I am in my twenties and, I hope, I have a long way still to go. I might look back on this in a few years or decades and think completely differently. I hope I do. I hope the world changes and I continue to grow too.

All I know for sure is how I got here and that this book needed to be written. It needed to be seen and read and it needed to be archived. The film director and gay rights activist Derek Jarman wrote, 'When I was young the absence of the past was a terror. That's why I wrote autobiography.'[1] Throughout the process of writing this, I have been aware of the lack of gay trans history that we have access to. I *know* it's out there because gay and trans people have always existed, even when political and societal structures have sought to erase us. So much has been destroyed. So I am aware that part of the reason I am writing now is so we can put ourselves in history.

Throughout my writing process, I struggled with putting too much of the hard stuff in. Too much violence and difficulty. I didn't want to give the impression that being gay

---

1   Lin, J. A. (2021) *Gay Bar: Why We Went Out.* London: Little, Brown. Epigraph.

and trans is only an uphill, high-gear struggle and that there is no joy to be found. I'm aware of the movement towards trans joy and a need to get away from the harshness of being trans. The representation of transness and trans joy is so important. But I also wanted to acknowledge that until we have true equality, transness cannot be entirely joyful for me. I wanted to be real to my experience and show that we can have trans joy and we can also experience violence. That we can have happy family relationships, but it doesn't mean it's always been that way. That although as LGBTQ+ people we are together, the fight has not ended. Between the gaps of violence there is so much joy in being real, finding who you are and feeling content with it. There is so much joy in gay love too. More than anything I wanted to bring up some of the stuff we face every single day. To archive our reality.

In this current moment, in 2023 in Britain, we are facing a call to remove the T from LGBT. This government are looking to remove conversion therapy for LGB people but exclude trans people. Trans people are having to withstand vicious and countless attacks from the media. Our press and newsfeeds are filled every day with debates about whether trans people are a danger to society. Whether we are terrorists, a major threat to children, and paedophiles. But no one is reporting about the dangers we face from the rest of society. Only yesterday, *BBC News* reported that transgender hate crimes are up by 87 per cent in Scotland.[2] I wanted to talk about that, as well as the nuances and interesting fiddly bits between gender and sexuality.

---

2   Clements, C. (2022) 'Transgender Hate Crimes Up 87% in Scotland.' *BBC News*, 14 June, 2022. Accessed on 20/09/2022 at www.bbc.co.uk/news/entertainment-arts-54447684

My writing and talking about being a gay and trans person in the UK today give me agency and power. So much of transness is about questioning what is real, and here I am on the page. In your hand. I am real. We exist.

When I look to gay and trans history, I find Lou Sullivan. I think it's one of those names that has been forgotten since he died of an AIDS-related illness in March 1991, but he is now starting to be remembered and recognized for the pioneer he was. He was refused testosterone by medical professionals on the basis that he liked men. Doctors at that time had a narrow view of what it meant to be trans, and so to 'become a man' Lou had to also be straight. Not willing to live another lie, Lou refused and is quoted as saying near the time of his death that if they weren't going to let him 'live as a gay man', he'd at least 'die like one'.[3] I read Lou's diaries recently, *Youngman: Selected Diaries of Lou Sullivan*, which only came out in 2021, a good few years after I was beginning my own gay and trans questioning. In his diaries, there was one extract which made me catch my breath. 'When people ask me at work "What do you want for yourself in the future?", how can I tell them that I just want to be a man?'[4] It reminded me so clearly of myself – of not being able to imagine or see a future past being male.

I – we – now get to live past Lou's future. We get to be the gay trans men and live openly in a way that Lou never could. So although progress is slow, it is happening. Now I have the opportunity to think about what my life looks like beyond being male and gay and I feel so lucky for that. I get

---

3   OurStories (1993) 'Lou Sullivan in His Own Words.' *OurStories 8*, 2, 6–7.
4   Sullivan, L. (2021) *Youngman: Selected Diaries of Lou Sullivan.* Ed. E. Martin and Z. Ozma. London: Vintage. p.209.

to imagine a future with holidays, family, pets, kids, jobs, reading, laughing and, I don't know – going to Tesco for a Meal Deal. The point is that a future beyond male is possible because I am living it. I can see past the limitations and gender and sexuality and be optimistic about whatever it is I might be able to achieve in the future. My very existence is proof of queer power and resistance.

Lou is also quoted as saying, 'I wanna look like what I am but don't know what someone like me looks like.'[5] It's been 32 years since his death date, and I am starting to see what people who are gay and trans look like, and I'm able to imagine endless possibilities of what we could be in the future. But in the meantime, I'm still searching to find people like me. With more publications, more listening, more sharing, I hope that we don't just have a few pictures or stories to look to. I hope that we have hundreds, thousands. We have been silenced for too long. It's time to make ourselves heard.

Now, as I finish writing this book, I'm in a much better place, albeit with different sorts of challenges. My transness and gayness stay with me – of course they do – and they make themselves known every day, but it's become more of a comfort than a challenge. Now my challenges look more like understanding my mental health, balancing friendships and workload, supporting my family and making sure I have enough coffee in for when they come round. Writing this book has been incredibly hard because there are so few blueprints for what it should look like – both for my life itself and for literature that shows gay transmasculine lives. At the same time, it has been cathartic looking back and seeing

---

5   Sullivan, L. (2021) *Youngman: Selected Diaries of Lou Sullivan*. Ed. E. Martin and Z. Ozma. London: Vintage. p.40.

how far I've come. How far we've all come. We have, finally, moved past the point of wanting to become male or female and not seeing any future beyond that. We recognize that trans people can love and be loved. Now I see hope and the possibility of us living more fully and freely. I must end on another quote from Lou Sullivan, as he puts it best:

> Oh God. I am so happy. My life as a gay man has been so fulfilling, so perfect, everything I could have hoped for. The beauty of a man loving a man just takes away my breath.[6]

Trans power and solidarity to you all and always.

---

6   Sullivan, L. (2021) *Youngman: Selected Diaries of Lou Sullivan*. Ed. E. Martin and Z. Ozma. London: Vintage. p.274.

Recommended Books

These books are a real mix. Partly because I couldn't decide on just a few essentials or just one genre – that would be like asking Tories to be kind and empathetic to trans people – impossible! But I've selected these and I've tried to be as concise as possible. A mini-queer bookshelf, if you like. They're a mix of trans and gay books because these encapsulate the themes of this book, and each has given me something in some way – be that help when I've needed it, a moment of recognition or learning something entirely new. I hope you find them equally as illuminating and insightful.

Non-fiction

Trans Love: An Anthology of Transgender and Non-Binary Voices – Edited by Freiya Benson

Queer Sex: A Trans and Non-Binary Guide to Intimacy, Pleasure and Relationships – Juno Roche

Trans Power: Own Your Gender – Juno Roche

Before We Were Trans: A New History of Gender — Kit Heyam

Trans Britain: Our Journey from the Shadows — Edited by Christine Burns

Straight Jacket — Matthew Todd

Gay Bar: Why We Went Out — Jeremy Atherton Lin

The Transgender Issue: An Argument for Justice — Shon Faye

The Appendix: Transmasculine Joy in a Transphobic Culture — Liam Konemann

Youngman: Selected Diaries of Lou Sullivan — Edited by Ellis Martin and Zach Ozma

Supporting Trans People of Colour: How to Make Your Practice Inclusive — Sabah Choudrey

None of the Above: Reflections on Life Beyond the Binary — Travis Alabanza

We Can Do Better Than This: 35 Voices on the Future of LGBTQ+ Rights — Edited by Ameila Abraham

Amateur: A True Story about What Makes a Man — Thomas Page McBee

Poetry

Physical — Andrew McMillan

The Backwater Sermons — Jay Hulme

100 Queer Poems: An Anthology — Edited by Mary Jean Chan and Andrew McMillan

The Man with Night Sweats – Thom Gunn

Limbic – Peter Scalpello

The Human Body Is a Hive – Erica Gillingham

Soho – Richard Scott

Nepantla: An Anthology Dedicated to Queer Poets of Color – Edited by Christopher Soto

Surge – Jay Bernard

Acknowledgements

Writing this book while in the middle of one of the most heated and polarizing 'debates' in British politics (and beyond), while simultaneously reckoning with the growing polarization of trans lives from within the LGBTQ+ community itself, has not been easy. I owe a huge amount of thanks to some incredible people.

To everyone at Jessica Kingsley Publishers – especially Andrew for his masterful editorial trickery and encouragement to 'delve deeper', especially when I found it hard. To Lily Bowden, Tamara Navaratnam, Sanphy Thomas and the rest of the JKP marketing team who support my endeavours on both sides of the publishing coin. Thanks also go to the Hachette Pride Network for supporting me and championing queer authors with such fierce tenacity. To Alison Barrow and Hilary Murray Hill for lifting me up and encouraging me to push higher.

Big thanks to my parents, Nigel and Janet, to whom this book is partially dedicated, for all your generosity, guidance, love and care.

Many thanks to my partner, Liam, who supports all of my dreams – not just the bookish ones. Thanks for supporting me while I wrote this book, fuelling me with endless mugs of tea, and for allowing me to stick Post-its all over our bedroom while I was trying to figure all this out. I will take them down now.

To Dean Austin for the chats, the laughs and the kick up the arse to stick to editorial deadlines.

I have to give special thanks to Alex Beighton, Alex Campbell, Arthur Webber, Catherine Lonergan, Dan Parkes, Elly Brookfield, Martin Conroy, Rosi Stamp, Tom Bailey and Samson Deitrich – all of whom have offered something to this book, whether that be in experience, friendship, advice, help or encouragement.

Thank you to Erica Gillingham and the team at Gay's the Word, who guided me gently into queer literary spaces. And to Andrew McMillan, who opened my world to gay masculinity through accomplished prose and allowed me to see myself on the page. And of course, to Travis Alabanza and Juno Roche, both of whom I've never met, but who have changed my life and perspective of gender in ways they cannot imagine.

And finally – thanks to you! For taking a risk and picking up this book. Love and trans power to you all.